Compulsory Education and the Amish

Compulsory Education and the Amish

The Right Not to Be Modern

Edited by Albert N. Keim

Beacon Press *Boston*

Beacon Press books are published under the auspices
of the Unitarian Universalist Association
Simultaneous publication in Canada by Saunders of Toronto, Ltd.

9 8 7 6 5 4 3 2 1

Grateful acknowledgment is made to the following for use of
material in this book:

The University of Chicago Press for "Showdown at an Amish
Schoolhouse," by Donald A. Erickson, from *Public Controls
for Nonpublic Schools*, Chicago, 1969, and "The Persecution
of LeRoy Garber," by Donald A. Erickson, from the journal
School Review, November 1969; the Lawyers Co-operative
Publishing Company for the United States Supreme Court
decision *Wisconsin* v *Yoder*; Pathway Publishers for "Who Shall
Educate Our Children?" by Joseph Stoll, Aylmer, Ontario, 1965;
Saturday Review / World for "Compulsory Education: The
Plain People Resist," by Stephen Arons, January 15, 1972.

Library of Congress Cataloging in Publication Data

Keim, Albert N
    Compulsory education and the Amish.
    Bibliography: pp. 187-203.
    Includes index.
    1. Education, Compulsory—United States.
2. Amish—Education—United States.   3. Educational
law and legislation—United States. I. Title.
LC131.K43   379'.23   74-16665
ISBN 0-8070-0500-2

In Memoriam
To Grant Stoltzfus,
Christian Scholar and
Champion of Religious Liberty

Contents

Preface

In the eyes of their secular contemporaries, the Old Order Amish seem a pastoral folk, immune from and oblivious to the "acids of modernity." It is true that the Amish have been one of America's most durable ethnic minorities. Their tightly knit community, horse-drawn economy, and primitivist theology have been buffeted by the forces of change, but their stubborn resistance to assimilation by American society continues.

The Amish do not, however, take their survival for granted. A focal point of their resistance to assimilation pressures has been compulsory public education. They have perceived, rightly so, it would appear, that public education represents a serious threat to their survival as a people. For more than fifty years there has been an ongoing skirmish between the Amish and public school authorities. The first recorded clash occurred in Ohio in 1914 when several Amish parents were jailed and fined for refusal to send their children to a newly consolidated school. Since then there have been numerous court cases over Amish refusal to honor school statutes. Prior to 1971, the courts found in favor of the Amish on only one occasion. In 1971 the Wisconsin Supreme Court reversed the decision of two lower courts and declared that the state education laws constituted an unjust restraint on Amish free exercise of religion. The State of Wisconsin appealed the decision to the U.S. Supreme Court in December 1971. The Court decided in favor of the Amish in May 1972.

This book illuminates the history of the Amish conflict with school authorities over the question of compulsory education and examines the implications of the most recent resolution of the problem in *Wisconsin* v. *Yoder et al.*

The essays by Pfeffer and Ball are edited versions of addresses delivered at a 1972 Symposium on "The Amish, Compulsory Education, and the Supreme Court." The symposium, sponsored by

Eastern Mennonite College, was attended by many of the principals involved in the Wisconsin school cases culminating in the Supreme Court decision.

I want to thank my colleagues, Professors Grant Stoltzfus, Gerald Brunk, and James Lehman, and the Dean of the College, Dr. Daniel Yutzy, for their advice and counsel in the editing of this volume.

Albert N. Keim

1

From Erlanbach to New Glarus

Albert N. Keim

Albert N. Keim is professor of history at Eastern
Mennonite College. Professor Keim was educated in
Amish parochial schools and is the son of an Amish
bishop. His grandfather was frequently fined in the 1920s
for his refusal to send Professor Keim's mother to
high school.

"From Erlanbach to New Glarus" is a brief historical
prologue to the recent Amish court cases.

Nestled in the rolling hills of Green County, Wisconsin, the
Swiss-American community of New Glarus achieved a modest
notoriety during the years 1968-1972. In 1968 public school
authorities clashed with a nearby community of Old Order Amish.
The Amish refused to send their children to the local high school
despite a Wisconsin law requiring attendance until sixteen years
of age. The school authorities insisted on compliance. The county
court upheld the school authorities. The case was eventually
appealed to the Wisconsin Supreme Court which rejected the
lower court decision and ruled that enforced schooling of Amish
children beyond the eighth grade was a violation of the free

exercise of the religious rights of the Amish. In 1972 the U.S. Supreme Court upheld the Wisconsin Supreme Court decision.

The Amish first arrived in the New Glarus area in 1963. By 1968 there were 24 Amish families in the community. The New Glarus Amish, who came from Ohio, Illinois, and Iowa, were part of a widespread migration of Amish people during the 1950s and 1960s. The motives for the migration were primarily economic: a search for cheap agricultural land. Urbanization and skyrocketing real estate values in the large and long-established Amish communities in Pennsylvania, Ohio, Indiana, and elsewhere, made Amish agricultural enterprise, particularly for young people, increasingly difficult. The rural counties of Wisconsin, where land prices were relatively low, saw a considerable influx of Amish farmers during the 1960s.

The Amish are one of America's last unassimilated ethnic groups. Their unusual costume and nonconformist lifestyle have obscured the fact, at least on the popular level, that these Protestant primitivists have proven to be highly successful community builders. In the twentieth century, however, the Amish community has encountered increasing difficulty in perpetuating itself. Its chief defenses have been a nineteenth-century technological agrarian economy, the German language, and the Ordnung. The latter is an unwritten, but comprehensive regulation of Amish life and practice.

Industrialism and urbanization have become an ever greater threat to the Amish, but perhaps nothing threatens the Amish community more than compulsory public education in modern consolidated schools. The Amish, almost instinctively, sense the potential for harm to their way of life in modern American schooling. The perception of the issues is often on the level of their sumptuary regulations. In the New Glarus case, one of the parents objected to her daughter's attendance in high school because she would be forced to wear shorts for physical education class, a serious violation of the Ordnung. Were the Amish to acquiesce on this point, an opening wedge would be made which in time would call into question other aspects of the Amish way of life.

For more than fifty years the Amish in the United States have been skirmishing with public school authorities. Before the New Glarus controversy, the conflict had been desultory and inconclusive. Here and there over the years school officials intent on enforcing the laws had encountered the Amish. Almost universally, when officials carried their case to the courts, they were upheld. The only case of a court finding in favor of the Amish was *Commonwealth* v. *Petersheim*, in Pennsylvania in 1950. Public opinion, however, often ran strongly in favor of the Amish, so that officials, especially elected officials, found it convenient to skirt the letter of the law and avoid controversy with the Amish by nonenforcement of the education laws.

On their part, the Amish, because of their religious objection to litigation, were reluctant to appeal their case to the courts. In countless instances over many years Amish refusal to obey compulsory attendance laws resulted in fines and short-term jailings. With few exceptions, they rejected recourse to legal process in self-defense. Frequently their response was migration to a locality where attendance laws were less rigorously enforced.

The Amish inability to comply with public education standards is rooted in their view of man's duty and destiny. "The purpose of Amish education," says attorney William Ball, "is not to get ahead in the world, but to get to heaven."[1] That perception of education grows out of a particular theological nexus and is conditioned by a unique historical experience.

The Amish are heirs of what has been called the "Anabaptist" or "Radical" wing of the Protestant Reformation of the sixteenth century. Anabaptism erupted in a variety of places during the Reformation, but the progenitors of the Amish originated in Zurich, Switzerland. There a small group of reformers, impatient with the gradualism of their leader, Ulrich Zwingli, created one of the first Anabaptist congregations in 1525.

The "Anabaptist Vision," as the late Professor Harold S. Bender aptly titled it, espoused adult baptism upon confession of faith, emphasized the visible, disciplined fellowship of believers as the locus of ethical and moral decision making, rejected participation in war, swearing of oaths and engaging in

litigation, and insisted on the ultimate authority of the New
Testament for faith and life.

The Anabaptist Vision spread rapidly for several decades
after 1525, carried by itinerant missioners often fleeing from
place to place to escape persecution from both civil and
religious authorities. By the 1530s the movement had spread
to the Netherlands in the west and Moravia in the east.
Persecution continued. Thousands were executed for their faith.
Martyrdom became the hallmark of Anabaptism.

In Switzerland persecution drove most Anabaptists, by
then called Swiss Brethren, into the valleys and highlands of
the Bernese Oberland. In the course of the seventeenth century,
while executions subsided, imprisonment and exile continued to
take their toll. The Bernese Swiss Brethren became refugees,
many of them fleeing to the Palatinate in Southwest Germany,
particularly during the heavy persecutions of the 1670s and
1690s. Others settled in Alsace on the frontier between France
and Germany. Numerous churches were formed there in the
seventeenth century. Those who remained in Switzerland moved
higher and higher into the Bernese highlands.

The persecution of the sixteenth and seventeenth centuries
profoundly altered the character of the Swiss Brethren. What had
begun as an urban movement became predominantly rural.
The aggressive evangelism of the early years subsided. The Swiss
Brethren became *die Stille im Lande* ("the quiet in the land").
Their enforced withdrawal to the periphery of society fostered
a strong group consciousness. Mutual aid, always an important
element in Anabaptist life, became not only a biblical duty,
but a physical necessity. Persecution intensified patterns of
group discipline.

Concern with a visible, disciplined, separate, and pure church
lay at the heart of original Anabaptism. One method by which
Anabaptists sought to maintain discipline was by means of the
"ban" or excommunication, a process based on Matthew 18,
and designed to exclude those unworthy of membership in the
body of Christ. The notion of the ban was included in the
Schleitheim Confession issued by the Swiss Brethren in 1527.
The principle was further elaborated a hundred years later in 1632

in the Dortrecht Confession of Faith, drawn up by Dutch
Anabaptists, by then known as Mennonites. The Dortrecht
Confession has since then become the essential statement of faith
for Mennonites and Amish. Article XVII dealt with the "shunning"
of those expelled from the church by excommunication. Those
expelled from the church were to be "shunned and avoided by
all the members of the church whether it be in eating or drinking,
or other social matters." Shunning was both a warning to the
faithful and a means of convicting the erring.

The Swiss Brethren had never practiced the strict application
of shunning as outlined in the Dortrecht Confession, although
some of the Swiss Brethren refugees in the Palatinate and Alsace
practiced a more rigid form, probably as a result of influence
from the Dutch Mennonites.

Jacob Amman of Erlanbach, Switzerland, a young Swiss
Brethren minister who apparently lived in Alsace for several years,
brought the more strict application of the ban to Switzerland
some time prior to 1693.

Amman became an articulate, if impulsive, proponent of the
ban and shunning. The application of the ban became the nub
of a controversy between Amman and an older bishop named John
Reist. At issue was the latter's refusal to excommunicate and
shun a member of the church who had confessed to telling an
untruth. Apparently Amman also sought to introduce two other
practices common to Alsace, but unfamiliar in Switzerland. These
were the observance of communion twice each year and the
practice of foot washing as an ordinance in connection with the
communion service.

In 1693 Amman and several other ministers toured Alsace
and Switzerland promoting these ideas. Upon their return to
Canton Bern they called a meeting of all Swiss Brethren ministers
to discuss the matter. Bishop Reist boycotted the meeting as he
did a later one in the summer of 1693. At the second meeting
Amman, apparently exasperated by Reist's refusal to discuss the
issues, read six charges against the older bishop and pronounced
him—and others who sided with him—excommunicated.

The followers of Amman began to meet separately and
subsequent efforts to heal the rift failed. Most of the churches in

Alsace and a few in the Palatinate and Switzerland followed
Amman. His followers came to be known as Amish Mennonites.

As the movement crystallized it developed distinctive
characteristics. The followers of Amman wore beards, emphasized
conservative and simple dress, and used hooks-and-eyes instead of
buttons on their clothing. They observed a strict application of
the ban or "Meidung." They developed a congregation centered
form of church polity, with great authority vested in the office
of bishop. In most other respects they shared Anabaptist
Mennonite theological ideas.

By 1700 the Amish had become a distinct subgroup within
the Anabaptist-Mennonite tradition. Forced migration and
resettlement was their lot in the eighteenth century. In 1712
Louis XIV expelled the Amish from Alsace. Many fled to the
Palatinate, Bavaria, and Baden. Usually they became tenant farmers
on the land holdings of noblemen, soon acquiring a reputation
as resourceful and excellent farmers. In Switzerland, harassment
continued, resulting in the migration of many Mennonites into
the Jura Mountains of northwestern Switzerland.

During the second and third decades of the eighteenth
century Amish immigrants began to arrive in Pennsylvania. By 1740
a sizable community settled in eastern Pennsylvania. During the
Napoleonic period, large numbers of Amish fled to America.
As more Amish arrived new settlements were established. Settlers
reached Fairfield and Holmes County, Ohio, by 1810. After the
War of 1812 the Amish followed the frontier west into Indiana,
Michigan, Illinois, and Iowa.

The nineteenth century was a critical period in the history
of the Amish. They arrived, like millions of other immigrants,
bearing the customs and culture of their homeland. Unlike many
of their fellows, the Amish were able to resist assimilation, and
in the course of the nineteenth century, created their own unique
communal and cultural structures. They became one of America's
few unassimilated immigrant groups.

The Amish came to America with a strong sense of group
consciousness, growing out of shared belief and common
experience. The shared belief was essentially the Anabaptist Vision
combined with the specific forms of church discipline and practice

resulting from the Amish schism of 1693-97. Religious persecution, ruralization, and forced migration, combined with South German-Swiss culture and language, constituted the common experience.

In short, the Amish came to America with a relatively well-defined and developed cultural heritage. In the course of the nineteenth century they created and crystallized a social structure to perpetuate the cultural heritage. Two elements were critical in this development. They created Amish communities and they developed an Ordnung by which to govern the life of their community.

The success of the Amish in building viable ongoing communities is a central factor in their ability to resist assimilation and survive as a group.[2] It is significant that those Amish who remained in Europe had rejoined the larger Mennonite Church or were assimilated by the end of the nineteenth century. The Amish in America were flourishing as never before at that point. One explanation is the Amish success in creating communities. Because of scarcity of land, and legal discrimination, and frequent forced migration, the Amish in Europe were never able to build viable communities. The family rather than the community served as the primary group. Consequently the Amish in Europe were much more continuously in contact with their non-Amish environment. The isolated families found it difficult to meet frequently with each other, or worship together; marriage with non-Amish occurred despite strictures against it; and, perhaps because of earlier persecution and continuing discrimination, the Amish tended to minimize the need to evangelize or gain new converts other than their own children. In the United States they were able, because of a ready supply of land and the absence of civil and legal discrimination, to create compact communities. Since the nineteenth century the Amish have been a communal people.

With the compact community as the setting, the Amish, over the course of the nineteenth century, proceeded to erect a social and cultural structure. This process was essentially the elaboration of the Ordnung—religious, sumptuary, and cultural—which came to govern the community. This Ordnung, cementing

the community into a cohesive whole, became the chief agent
in defending the Amish against assimilation.

What prompted the Amish concern with Ordnung? Why did
they develop such a rigid and detailed scheme of direction?
The Amish in early America faced the problems of all immigrants
to the U.S. confronted by the malleable, unformed, eclectic
character of American society and culture. For the Amish the
greatest challenge lay in learning to practice their faith in an
environment of religious freedom. Their theology and church life
had been hammered out on the anvil of religious persecution. Now
they faced the problem of making that theology and practice
viable in the new context.

They came to the New World with a deep-seated conviction
that Christians must be, in biblical terms, "a peculiar people."
"Be not conformed to this world" and "Be ye not unequally
yoked together with unbelievers" were phrases reinforced by
both Amish biblical literalism and religious persecution. For the
Amish in Europe this concept had been more a spiritual than a
sociological reality. They had not, for example, developed a
distinctive clothing style, except for their focus on simplicity.
Upon coming to America they became conscious of their dress
in relation to their frontier non-German neighbors, and in the
course of time discovered that in the absence of religious
persecution or civil disabilities, the South German clothing styles
were a form of protective identity in the new environment.
They, in effect, traditionalized the dress styles which they brought
to America from Europe. The beard, the hooks-and-eyes, the
mutze (dress coat), the black wide-rimmed hats, the broad-fall
trousers, the Halsduch and schatz (cape and apron), and the
prayer cap were all common dress styles of the eighteenth-century
Palatine, Alsatian, and Swiss areas.

By the end of the nineteenth century the Amish had worked
out a general consensus regarding what constituted a proper
Ordnung. There are extant Ordnungs of 1809, 1837, and 1865,[3]
which reflect the concerns of the Amish to maintain their identity
as a separate people. The Discipline of 1865, for example, makes
the following statements regarding sumptuary regulations:

> *Next:* Decided not to allow attendance at worldly
> conventions, or fairs, or yearly fairs, or to take part in
> them, or to enroll our material possessions in companies
> [insurance?], or to put up lightning rods on our buildings.
> Likewise, decided not to allow gayly-colored ["scheckich"],
> striped, or flowered clothing made according to the fashions
> of the world, or parting the hair of man or woman after the
> wordly styles, or cutting the beard according to worldly
> styles, or carrying hidden on one's person photographic
> pictures of human likenesses or hanging them on the wall
> to look at in our houses. Likewise it is not allowed to
> wear overcoats made of oilcloth or rubber or other
> overcoats made according to the worldly styles, likewise
> false shirt bosoms, likewise merchandising after the worldly
> fashion, for the Saviour drove such out of the temple.
> Likewise, luxurious vehicles according to the world's pride
> and vanity.[4]

Another powerful deterrent to assimilation was the German
language. By maintaining German as the language of its key
community activity, worship, the Amish cemented community and
culture into a highly impregnable whole. The German langauge,
even in its Pennsylvania Dutch form, has remained the single
most significant element in the continuity of the Amish
community. It is doubtful whether the community could survive
its loss.

On the other hand, without the community, it is doubtful
that the language could have survived, for its propagation was
almost totally dependent on oral transmission. In the twentieth
century some Amish communities have instituted Sunday schools
whose purpose is not Bible study, but German language study,
using the Luther Bible as a textbook.

Another factor which has promoted the self-consciousness
of the Amish and fostered social and cultural legislation within
the community has been the presence of Mennonites in proximity
to Amish communities. The presence of the parent group kept
alive the issues which prompted the original schism. The key
issue has been the question: shall members who join the Mennonite

Church be banned in domestic relations or only at the communion table? The presence of Mennonites exacerbated the issue throughout Amish history in America, for Amishmen, especially the young, have defected to the Mennonite Church in large numbers.

As the Amish Ordnung became more explicit, a new rationale for it also developed, not superseding the earlier "peculiar people" concept, but supplementing it, and, in effect, legitimating the Ordnung as an essentially defensive device protecting the community from external pressures. The Ordnung came to be known as a *Zaun* ("a fence") against the world. Bishop David O. Treyer of Ohio reflected the notion of the *Zaun* in his book of sermons and admonitions written in 1870.

> First [he says,] it should be noted that all Christian churches must be fenced-in ("um zäunt") with rules and regulations which are based and grounded on God's Word. For without such a spiritual fence no church can long survive. Where no Christian "Ordnung" exists, God cannot be served. Therefore, observe dear children, that it is always necessary to maintain this fence (Zaun) in God's Church, just as one does in a vineyard. . . .[5]

The Amish Ordnung became more detailed as time went on, and as it grew more explicit, agreement on its details became more and more difficult. By the 1860s the differences regarding the Ordnung became so serious that annual ministers' conferences were held to preserve unity of practice. Some were held in Ohio, others in Pennsylvania. Ministers attended from as far west as Iowa. The ministers' conferences failed in their purpose, however, and by the 1870s two broad Amish factions were discernible.

A "progressive" group, which resisted the strict application of the Ordnung, eventually gravitated to the Mennonite Church and by 1900 had become largely affiliated with that church. The conservative group, which after 1860 came to be known as "Old Order Amish," insisted on the strict application of the Meidung and the Ordnung. It is they who are today the bearers of the legacy of Jacob Amman.

In their nineteenth-century community building the Amish

made virtually no effort to create educational institutions. Their
agrarian economy, combined with a suspicion that worldly learning
was subversive of godliness, militated against educational initiatives.
From the evidence, the Amish educated their children as well
or as poorly as the average rural population in the nineteenth
century. Bishop David Beiler, writing in 1861, reflected this in
his memoirs: " . . . one did not go to school every winter for
months at a time. One was satisfied with learning to read and
write. It was considered that for the humble state or for the
common man more was not necessary."[6]

Most Amish children attended the public schools available
in their communities. Such schooling became more prevalent
as the number of public schools increased in the last half of the
century. Even the rudimentary public education offered at the
time did not please all Amishmen. As early as the 1860s the
Amish in Pennsylvania objected to attendance in public schools.
An Amishman writing in 1882 expressed fear that the Amish
were too sanguine in their acceptance of public education for
their children. He criticized the existing view of child training
by public educators. "Such a viewpoint," he said, "belongs to
the materialistic spirit of the present age."[7] A pioneer in the
promotion of Amish-German church schools, Samuel D. Guenerich
of Iowa, made what has since become a key Amish criticism of
public education:

> The righteousness that counts before God is neither
> sought nor found in the public or free schools; they are
> interested only to impart worldly knowledge, to ensure
> earthly success and to make good citizens for the state.[8]

Despite such reservations, the Amish continued to attend
public schools. As long as public schools were rural, locally
controlled, and reflected the general Protestant ethic, the Amish
were content to allow their children to attend them. Overt
conflicts between the Amish and education authorities are a
twentieth-century phenomenon, arising from Amish awareness
that new educational initiatives are vitiating the nineteenth-
century character of public schools.

Significantly, the Amish were defining and establishing themselves as an ethnic group at the same time that state departments of education were developing comprehensive new school systems. By the time most states had legislated compulsory attendance statutes, the Amish Ordnung had been defined and the Amish community was consciously at variance with the urbanizing secularizing tendencies of the larger society.

From the time of the formation of the United States, it has been assumed that popular government requires a literate public. Thomas Jefferson was an early and forceful advocate of the legality and necessity of widespread public education. During much of the nineteenth century, however, Jefferson's vision of a universal educational system was not effectively brought into being. Toward the end of the century many states enacted compulsory attendance laws, but for the most part the laws were not well enforced, due to inertia, desire to profit from child labor, and reluctance to interfere in what many believed to be a domestic matter.

A Massachusetts law of 1852 set the pattern for others later in the century. It required school attendance between the ages of eight and fourteen years for a period of twelve weeks each year. Attendance was to be continuous for six weeks. But the law was not enforced. Ohio passed an attendance law in 1877 but failed to include provisions for the prosecution of offenders.

After 1890 enforcement of compulsory attendance laws began to take place. Progressive educators, prompted partly by a desire to "Americanize" the large numbers of immigrants pouring into the country, pressed for more comprehensive laws and more aggressive enforcement of the laws. Ignorance, argued B. G. Northrop of the Connecticut Board of Education, should be stamped out, because it is a chief cause of crime. Not only does government have the responsibility to punish crime, it must prevent it. Education is society's most effective means of prevention.[9]

Several court cases vindicated the constitutionality of compulsory schooling, on the grounds of "welfare of the minor" and that education safeguards the welfare of the community and the safety of the state. The institution of a school census, adopted widely about 1900, made enforcement of school statutes more effective. After 1905, with restrictions on child labor, compulsory attendance laws were tightened and the upper age limit extended. In short, after the turn of the century, and particularly after 1920, the rise in the compulsory attendance age, combined with more aggressive enforcement of attendance laws, brought the public schools into conflict with the Amish.

Two additional elements entered the American educational scene after 1900. One was consolidation of schools; the other, secondary education. Both were perceived by the Amish as threats to their way of life.

Secondary education grew rapidly after 1900. Between 1890 and 1940 total enrollment of high schools nearly doubled every decade.[10] Between 1913 and 1922 a Commission on Reorganization of Secondary Education, chaired by Clarence Kingsley and working under the auspices of the National Education Association, published sixteen reports on the reorganization of the high school. The most significant report was entitled *Cardinal Principles of Secondary Education*, issued in 1918. It broadened the aims of secondary education and recommended the comprehensive high school. The report was a blueprint for a new, uniquely American secondary school designed to serve all American youth in a democratic industrial society.[11]

The Amish response to the high school was that for the Amish child it was irrelevant; it did not enhance the prospects of salvation. In fact, worldly knowledge, represented by the high school, could impair salvation.

But the advent of the high school was made even less desirable in Amish eyes by the process of consolidation. The various rationales for consolidation need no elaboration here, except for one raised by Robert J. Alley in 1910 which touches on a central area of conflict between the Amish and the American educational community. Said Alley:

> . . . [O]ne of the greatest factors in favor of the consolidated school is that it enlarges the neighborhood. Instead of the old district unit of four square miles it gives a larger unit of twenty or thirty square miles. By means of this larger unit

the petty jealousies and narrow prejudices of the old
smaller unit are broken down. All the children of this larger
unit become acquainted and thus enlarge their horizons.[12]

Alley voiced precisely what the Amish fear most. They
understand quite clearly that expanding the horizons of their
children threatens their loyalty to the Amish community, for
the Amish community is what it is by a willful constriction of
horizons. What appears liberating to Alley strikes at the very
roots of Amish life, for without the community there can be
no Amishmen. Bishop D. D. Miller had this in mind when he
observed that the "Amish fear the public schools will melt all men
into one and thereby destroy or fatally weaken the Amish
Church."[13]

The Amish resisted consolidation because it weakened
parental authority over their children. Nineteenth-century one-room
public schools could be tolerated because the children were
within the ambit of the local community where relatively direct
control over activities and teachers was possible. The Amish take
parental responsibility very seriously, for like everything else in
their lives, it has ultimate religious implications. What parents
do for their children, writes an Amishman, "may well influence
their entire life and determine where they will spend eternity."[14]

Finally, consolidation appeared to the Amish as a major
threat because it often ushered in new curricula and, in their
view, faulty pedagogical methods. The Amish view education as
a way to encourage the child to follow instructions, respect
authority, and master basic information. They are skeptical of
education which stresses engagement, critical thinking, or asking
questions. They favor rote learning. The community can survive
only if authority and tradition are respected and upheld.

The conjunction, therefore, of compulsory attendance laws,
secondary education reform, and consolidation created conditions
which inevitably led to conflict. The point of controversy has
nearly always been the Amish refusal to honor compulsory
attendance laws which require consolidated high school attendance.

The first conflict on record occurred in Geauga County,
Ohio, in 1914, a conflict which, significantly, coincided with the

reorganization of the Ohio public school system. Three Amishmen
were fined because they kept their children out of school in
violation of the new school statutes.[15] Subsequently, particularly
in the 1920s and 1930s, Amish frequently suffered fines and
jail sentences for failure to observe the school attendance laws.
Usually this was in connection with a youngster who, in Ohio for
example, finished the eighth grade before his sixteenth birthday.

The Amish have been surprisingly slow at setting up parochial
schools. The first school was established in 1925 in Delaware,
and in the 1930s a number of schools were begun in Pennsylvania.
The g eatest interest in Amish parochial schools has come since
World War II. Postwar educational reform, notably in the area of
curriculum, but also in terms of methodology, has upset the
Amish. Coincidentally, the Amish themselves have become more
aware of the importance of parochial education, prompted in
part by the large number of small Amish settlements established
since World War II. These new communities, the outgrowth of a
search for cheap land and concern for reform of the Ordnung,
are usually highly conscious of their identity, surrounded as they
are by a strange environment. Frequently one of the first acts
of these communities is the creation of a parochial school.

The Amish parochial school did not resolve the problem of
compulsory attendance laws, for in most states the minimum
school leaving age still required attendance at a high school for
one or more years. This most Amish continued to resist. It
was this issue which led to conflict in New Glarus, Wisconsin.
The Supreme Court decision in *Wisconsin* v. *Yoder et al.* (1972)
has finally, after many decades of litigation and travail, given the
Amish surcease from the strictures of compulsory education beyond
the eighth grade.

2

Who Shall Educate Our Children?

Joseph Stoll

Joseph Stoll is a thirty-eight-year-old Amish writer and teacher who has been a leader in the Amish parochial school movement. Born in Indiana, he spent most of his life in an Amish community in Ontario, Canada. Recently he and his family emigrated to British Honduras. He served for many years as editor of *The Blackboard Bulletin*, an Amish parochial school journal which gave important direction and cohesiveness to the Amish parochial school movement in the 1960s.

In "Who Shall Educate Our Children?" Stoll very effectively summarizes the basic attitudes of the Amish toward public education.

WHAT ARE THE DUTIES OF CHRISTIAN PARENTS?

In today's world, Christian parents are in a difficult position. In a sense, this is nothing new. There have always been problems. But in many ways, our age is not to be compared to former ones, for the twentieth century has troubles peculiar to itself.

In the early days of the Christian church, and again in the

days of our Anabaptist forefathers, the powers of darkness ruled in fury. Thousands of devout believers were martyred for their faith.

It was not easy to be a parent in time of persecution. One or both of the parents were frequently placed in prison, or executed. We have several letters in *The Martyrs Mirror* from parents in prison to their children. These touching letters show clearly the deep concern they felt for the welfare of their children. This concern for their orphaned children was one of the sharpest thorns of a martyr's crown.

The parents of our day faces the same foe, but the Enemy has changed his tactics. The Bible describes Satan as both "a roaring lion," and as one who poses as "an angel of light." Today in our country we have not experienced the persecution of former years. Satan, instead, comes to us in a subtle way, setting before us enticing temptations, or bringing about changes so gradually, that we are not aware of what is happening until it is too late.

This is not to say that persecution is out of date. Christians in other lands have been severely persecuted, and thousands martyred, in the last twenty years. It is not at all impossible, nor even improbable, that we too may yet have to stand for our faith, even unto death.

We do not know what the future holds for us and our children, but we do know Who holds the future. Were it not for this consolation, the uncertainties of the years ahead would be even more frightening.

As parents we are challenged with rearing our children to serve God. There are many things to hinder us, and Satan has set many snares. But the outlook is not hopeless, if we are willing to do what is required of us, and seek help from the Lord. "(His) hand is not shortened, that it cannot save; neither his ear heavy, that it cannot hear" (Isaiah 59:1).

But we must meet the requirements if we expect God to help us. The Bible clearly states what are the duties of parents. If we neglect these duties, how can we expect His blessings?

Years ago the Lord had the following to say of Abraham: "For I know him, that he will command his children and his

household after him, and they shall keep the way of the Lord,
to do justice and judgment."

Likewise, the Israelites were instructed to diligently keep
the commandments of the Lord, "and teach them to your children,
speaking of them when thou sittest in thine house, and when
thous walkest by the way, when thou liest down, and when thou
risest up."

Solomon, the wisest of the kings, has much to say on the
training of children. Perhaps the best known of his sayings is
Proverbs 22:6, "Train up a child in the way he should go:
and when he is old, he will not depart from it."

In the New Testament we read Paul's advice to parents,
"And, ye fathers, provoke not your children to wrath: but
bring them up in the nurture and admonition of the Lord"
(Ephesians 6:4).

Teaching, commanding, training, bringing them up, these
are the duties of parents to their children. But we might ask
ourselves a question. Are we training and teaching our children,
if we send them to state schools five days a week? Is not the
state training them then? One writer has said:

> I never read anywhere in the New Testament that
> the church is supposed to expect the state to educate our
> children. When this country was founded, all education
> was parochial school education, that is, controlled by the
> church. Is it any wonder that so many of our youth go
> astray when they are educated by the state for five days
> a week and by the church for two hours a week?[1]

It is the concern of this writing to state the case for church
schools, explaining why they are necessary, what is involved,
and what to do about it. May the Lord bless the efforts of all
concerned parents who seek the will of God in this matter.

THE RECORD OF HISTORY

Perhaps the greatest military general of all time, Napoleon
Bonaparte, made the profound statement, "Public instruction

should be the first object of government." Why should Napoleon say something like this? Always through history the responsibility of education had lain at the doorsteps of the church and the home. Why should the Emperor of France want this responsibility turned over to the state?

The answer lies in the changes brought about by the Protestant Reformation. The Roman Catholic Church had held, and still holds, that education is a religious responsibility. But Luther and the Calvinists urged universal education under *state control.* This was not as great a change as might be supposed, for they maintained a union of church and state, but it did do one thing. It marked the first step by the Protestant churches to turn education entirely over to the state.

By the time of Napoleon, the idea of public education had gained favor, but it was not until the late nineteenth and early twentieth centuries that it reached fulfillment. A program of state-supported and state-controlled education was introduced in the United States by Horace Mann during the second quarter of the nineteenth century. It was not generally accepted until after 1850. In other words, public schools as we know them are little more than a century old.

By contrast, church or parochial schools in some form or other have existed for many centuries. An article on schools in the Smith-Peloubet Bible Dictionary gives us some facts concerning elementary school training in Bible times.

In the early ages most of the instruction of young children was by the parents. The leisure hours of the Sabbaths and festival days brought the parents in constant contact with the children. After the captivity, schools came more into use, and at the time of Christ were very abundant. The schools were in connection with the synagogues, which were found in every city and in almost every village of the land. Their idea of the value of schools may be gained from such sayings from the Talmud as, "The world is preserved by the breath of the children in the schools. A town in which there are no schools must perish. Jerusalem was destroyed because the education of children was neglected."

Josephus says, "Our principal care is to educate our children." Maimonides thus describes a school: "The teacher sat at the head and the pupils surrounded him as the crown the head, so that every one could see the teacher and hear his words. The teacher did not sit in a chair while the pupils sat on the ground, but all either sat on chairs or on the ground. The chief studies were their own language and literature, the chief school book the Holy Scriptures; and there were special efforts to impress lessons of morality and chastity."[2]

In the year of 200 A.D., the Christians of Alexandria had a school where the children were given instruction in the Christian faith. These schools are thought to have been founded in the days of the Apostles. We read of children ten to twelve years old attending the school of Alexandria.

Down through the ages, there were always minority groups that were strict Biblicists, holding to the faith "once delivered to the saints." These groups, such as the Waldensians and the Albigenses, had a great zeal for learning and knowing the Scriptures. Of the Waldensians, John Horsch writes:

Bibles were not plentiful before the invention of printing, but of the Waldensians it may be said that for their use of the Scriptures they were to a considerable degree independent of the possession of copies of the Bible. They followed the usage of committing large portions of the Scriptures to memory. Many members of the Waldensian Church could recite whole books of the Bible from memory. Even such as were not able to read knew some of the most precious parts of the Scriptures by rote.[3]

During the early days of Anabaptism in Europe, organized parochial schools were almost impossible. The heavy hand of persecution kept the brethren from publicly establishing schools. But the Anabaptists were not slack in teaching their children and new converts to read and write. In the homes, or in small groups secretly, the young were taught their letters, so that they could understand the Bible, admonish each other, and help spread the Gospel message.

A lengthy debate in 1559 between Friar Cornelis, a Catholic monk, and the Anabaptist Jacob de Roore is recorded in *The Martyrs Mirror.*

"Before you are rebaptized," said the monk, "you can't tell A from B, but as soon as you are baptized, you can read and write. If the devil has not a hand in this, I do not understand anything about you people."

"I can well hear you do not understand our way of doing," replied Jacob, "for you ascribe to Satan the grace which God grants our simple converts when we with all diligence teach them to read."

The Anabaptists thought it was necessary to learn to read and write, but they did not think the schools of the state church were the proper place for their children to learn these skills. For over a century the Swiss Brethren of the Canton of Schaffhausen suffered various forms of persecution, fines, loss of property, and banishment. One measure was to forcibly take the children to Reformed Church services and schools. We read that, as late as 1648, the Anabaptists refused to send their children to school and to church. The government then took over their farms and possessions and ordered them to leave.

The Dutch Mennonites who moved to Prussia and later to Russia were the leaders in setting up well-organized church schools. Horsch, in *Mennonites in Europe*, relates the following:

> In the year 1737, King August II of Poland published a manifesto stating that the Mennonites had been called into the country to clear and bring into cultivation the swampy wastelands of the region, and they had given proof of their expert knowledge of the most practical methods for accomplishing this task. For this reason, the manifesto stated further, they were granted the privilege of freely practicing their religion, of holding religious services in private homes and other places, of having their own schools with teachers of their own communion, of instructing and baptizing their own youth, and so forth.[4]

These same rights were granted by the Russian government when a large group of Prussian immigrants settled on the steppes of Russia, beginning in 1789. These immigrants brought with them the conviction that it is the duty of parents to provide for the elementary instruction of their children. The Mennonites set up their own villages, and each village had its own school. These schools were well planned, and by World War I had reached a high state of development. With a total population of about 110,000, the Mennonites of Russia had about 450 elementary schools in 1920, with 16,000 pupils.

The schools of the Russian Mennonites were definitely church schools, and not mere private schools to teach the secular subjects. Religion was always one of the principal subjects of instruction. A statement to the government officials at St. Petersburg in 1870 made clear the Mennonite position on this:

> Both the village and secondary schools . . . must have absolutely the character of church schools, and only if they are confirmed as such do they fulfill their purpose, since in these schools not only our teachers, who must also be the religious instructors of our children, but also our preachers and pastors must be trained. All schools under us must be so definitely founded on the Mennonite Confession that the students can acquire a religious training that will qualify them to assume the office of a preacher or an elder, for according to our organization and the Holy Scriptures, these officials must be chosen from among the people.[5]

The Mennonites brought this high regard for parochial schools with them when they began a migration to Canada in the 1870s. The Canadian government granted them the privilege of operating their schools on the same plan as in Russia. But, following World War I, the Manitoba Department of Education took steps to replace the Mennonite schools with public schools. This resulted in wholesale emigration of the Old Colony Mennonites, the most conservative group in Canada, to Mexico and Paraguay during the years 1922-27. In Mexico today, the

Old Colony settlers live in villages and have their own schools and self-government exactly as their forefathers did over a century ago in Russia.

In colonial Pennsylvania the early Mennonites established schools in their communities, but these were usually private subscription schools. Often school was held in the local church. Silas Hertzler states that by 1776, at least sixteen schools were being conducted by the Mennonite groups in Pennsylvania. The noted teacher, Christopher Dock, taught such a school in the first half of the 1700s.

The public school system was not introduced a century ago without some notable opposition. Dr. A. A. Hodges said, "I am as sure as I am of the fact of Christ's reign that a comprehensive and centralized system of national education, separated from religion, as is now commonly proposed, will prove the most appalling enginery for the propagation of anti-Christian and atheistic unbelief, which this sin-rent world has ever seen."

Though there were voices raised against state-controlled education, it appears that the Amish and Mennonites in general accepted the plan without protest. This was especially true in the central and western states where the settlers were scattered and poor. Here church schools had been largely neglected. The children were not being taught what was needed to make a living, or to read the Bible. When the government began to establish schools, the Amish and the Mennonites were glad for the opportunity afforded their children to obtain "booklarnin" during the idle winter months. The program at the outset may have appeared harmless enough. Attendance was not compulsory.

But before the end of the century, many leaders became alarmed at what was happening. Attendance laws gradually drew more and more children into the schools, and kept them there for longer and longer terms. The churches began to realize what they had lost when they turned education over to the state. An anonymous writer lamented in an article to the *Herold der Wahrheit* magazine in 1882:

> [There is] great anxiety because there are no Christian schools in these parts where one can with a good conscience

send his children. Many of our dear brethren . . . seem to think
think the existing public schools are sufficient and quite
satisfactory. . . . Their understanding of child-training
reflects the commonly-accepted but shallow, views of the
American people. . . . Such a viewpoint belongs to the
materialistic spirit of the present age.

Earnest and thinking Christians cannot and will not
approve of sending their children to these schools to be
educated. Not only are they a true likeness of the popular
churches, but frequently they are the very hotbeds of the
kingdom of darkness. For whosoever is even in a small
measure familiar with the spirit that rules in the public
schools, and compares it with the Biblical command to
bring up our children in the nurture and admonition of
the Lord—such a person must admit that the true Christian
cannot, with respect to the training of his children, walk
hand in hand with the world, for if one allows his children
to go to the worldly schools, how can he expect anything
else than that his child will later go to the worldly churches?

I want to now make a suggestion how our brotherhood
may overcome this tragic situation, namely, by establishing
church schools, that is, private schools in which brothers
of the church are the teachers. It is evident that this will
mean a sacrifice of money if the church is to build a
school house, buy supplies, and hire a teacher. But where
are the parents who should not be willing to make this
sacrifice for their children?[6]

Similarly, an Amish writer, publisher, and lay leader, Samuel
D. Guengerich of Johnson County, Iowa, wrote in 1896:

Many a well-meaning friend will say, "If we must pay
the tax anyway, to support the public schools, then I want
to send my children there. Otherwise, I will receive no
benefit from it."

This I will not try to contradict. We believe that the
lessons taught in public schools have their worth in that
for which they are intended, namely, to prepare a person

to make a living. But, if our children are sent only to these public schools, their minds will be so saturated with this world's wisdom that little room will be left for Christianity. Nor will they have a desire for it. Then will the Christian life, yes, the better part, which Mary chose, be given second place. Yet the Bible plainly says that we are to seek first the kingdom of God, and set our affection on things above, not on things of the earth.

Once a generation of such children has grown up, we will find many of them believing it is enough to have an outward form, and thinking it most important to provide their children with earthly possessions. But, my dear friends, this does not agree with God's Word. For, as we have shown above, our duty is to seek first the kingdom of God and the well-being of our souls. The righteousness which counts before God is neither sought nor found in the public or free schools; they are intended only to impart worldly knowledge, to ensure earthly success, and to make good citizens for the state.[7]

S. D. Guengerich took the lead in Iowa to found several German schools, or *"Deutsche Gemeinde Schulen,"* as they called them. The above words were written in 1896, and for a decade or two, we find winter German schools were fairly common among the Amish groups from Pennsylvania to Iowa and Kansas. These schools had two objectives, to teach German and to teach the message of the Bible. Only too often the latter aim was lost sight of in pursuit of the former, but all the same, these German schools were our first attempt in recent times to educate our own children. They continued for three or four months during the winter, and the pupils were often divided into grades, or classes, quite similar to our elementary schools today. The greatest difference was in the subjects being taught.

Abraham S. Yoder of Belleville, Pennsylvania, taught at least five terms of these German schools. He writes, "In the year 1902, a German school was organized [in Big Valley] . . . and I was asked to be the teacher. I was paid five cents a day per pupil, and I would furnish the fuel."[8]

The following year the same writer states,

> When we arrived in the Middlefield section, the Amish
> folks had learned that I had taught German school. So friends
> in Troy Township asked me to teach for them in a building
> on the Peter W. Swartzentruber premises, which offer I
> accepted. They paid me twenty dollars a month, and I
> helped with the chores and worked Saturdays for my board
> and lodging, all of which I appreciated.[9]

During the next two winters, Mr. Yoder again taught
German school near Belleville, and he writes that in the summer
of 1907, "I received a letter from Amish friends in Madison
County, Ohio, asking me to teach German school three months
for them. Sensing the need, and the employment out of the
weather, I accepted. This school in Madison was held in a vacant
country schoolhouse. A little over 40 scholars attended."[10]

In a few communities these schools have survived until
the present, but on the whole they lasted only a few years.
Because of longer compulsory school terms, the German classes
of today usually are for only a few weeks, squeezed into the
Christmas holidays, or during the summer. In a few instances,
German schools are held for those pupils through the regular
school.

As we have noted, several Amish and Mennonite writers
tried hard to promote parochial schools before 1900. But no
full-fledged elementary school came into being until January 1925,
when the Apple Grove School, near Dover, Delaware, first opened
its doors for classes.

According to Samuel Hertzler, first secretary for the school,
and one of its leading supporters, construction on the school
building was begun in October of 1924, and the school was ready
for classes in January. It was founded mainly to evade the state's
move toward consolidation. Grades seven and eight, in particular,
were to be taken to the high school in Dover. This move the
Amish opposed, and they finally decided to open a school of their
own. In this they succeeded, with the cooperation of public
school officials.

For thirteen years Apple Grove was the only Amish parochial school in existence. The neighboring Mennonite settlement at Greenwood, Delaware, opened a school in 1928. But the second Amish school was to be Green Hill, also at Dover, in 1938. This was the same year, however, that Pennsylvania's first Amish school was opened.

Since that time, and especially in the last ten years, new Amish schools have been going up each year in widely scattered communities. Today Ohio leads the states, with almost seventy schools; Pennsylvania has forty; and Indiana, fifteen. Missouri has ten schools; New York, five; Wisconsin and Ontario, each three. Michigan, Iowa, Delaware, and Tennessee have two schools each.

In some of these states the Amish had a legal struggle obtaining permission to operate their own schools. There are indications that the worst is now past, and in those states where Amish schools already exist, very little "red tape" is encountered in establishing a new school.

WHAT IS WRONG WITH PUBLIC SCHOOLS?

This is a good question. And the answer is a long one. Not only is the very idea of the state educating our children unsound, there are many other angles to consider. Children from other types of homes—godless, atheistic, materialistic, of false cults—have an un-Christian influence on our children. Teachers who do not share our Christian faith can lead a child astray. There are many harmful influences we can avoid by maintaining our own schools, but this is only half the story. The other half is the positive side, the good we can teach our children in church schools, which they are not taught in public schools.

What is wrong with public schools? First, the idea is foreign to everything the Bible teaches and our forefathers practiced in the line of separation from the world.

Paul was educated at the feet of Gamaliel, the famous Jewish teacher. But can we picture Paul, after his conversion, admonishing the Christians to send their young men to Gamaliel to be taught? Or can we imagine him speaking to the Christian parents at Athens, or in any of the other heathen cities where he labored, advising them to have their children educated in one of the foremost schools of Greece?

What did Menno Simons and other Anabaptist leaders teach and write on the training of children? Let us remember that it was the alliance of state and church that brought them persecution and martyrdom. Therefore, teaching and training was the responsibility of the parents and brethren of the church. Menno Simons wrote in 1557:

> The world desires for its children that which is earthly and perishable, money, honor, fame and wealth. From the cradle they rear them to wickedness, pride, and idolatry. But let it be otherwise with you, who are born of God, for it behooves you to seek something else for your children, namely, that which is heavenly and eternal, so that you may bring them up in the nurture and admonition of the Lord as Paul teaches.
>
> Moses commanded Israel to teach their children the law and commandments of the Lord, to talk of them when they sat down in their houses and when they walked by the way, when they lay down, and when they rose up. Now since we are the chosen generation, the royal priesthood, the holy nation, the peculiar people, that we should show forth the praises of Him who hath called us out of darkness unto His marvelous light, therefore we ought to be patterns and examples in all righteousness and blamelessness, and to manifest this to the whole world as we are called to this. . . . For this is the chief and principal care of the saints, that their children may fear God, do right and be saved.[11]

How can we parents expect our children to grow up untainted by the world, if we voluntarily send them into a worldly environment, where they associate with worldly companions, and are taught by men and women not of our faith six hours a day, five days a week, for the greater part of the year? Yet we have grown so accustomed to this state of affairs that we hardly give it a thought.

We persist in thinking of ourselves as being a light to the world, a witness to the unrighteous. At the same time, we allow the world to teach and train our children! Brethren, where is our discernment? One writer has said,

> This nation would consider utterly ridiculous the idea of sending its soldiers to Russia to be trained in order to later fight that nation. Just so, it is ridiculous to have children trained in the world to combat the forces of evil.[12]

What is wrong with public schools? Second, the companions and environment are not Christian. Children have a great influence on each other. It is natural for a child to want to be recognized, and to seek the approval and admiration of his playmates. It is important to "belong," and in order to be accepted, a child must to a certain degree conform to the standards of the group. He must have the same interests, and share in the activities.

This tendency to conform is a help in a church school where standards are high, and the children come from Christian homes. But the opposite is true when the children are from worldly homes. The influence the companions of our children have on them is much greater than we may realize.

In the small one-room country schools of yesteryear, this matter of companions was not so important as it is today. It was important even then, but today, with larger schools, there is much greater possibility of harmful influences entering the school. With the small schools, all the parents were known to each other, and they could cooperate in keeping a school decent, even though they were not of like faith. In a large consolidated school, this is difficult.

And what are the interests and standards of the average child today? What does he talk about with his companions when no one else is listening? Adults are not included in the "inside circle," so I can only speak from my own experience when I was in school. From the age of six until I was sixteen, I attended five different public schools, and I have since heard others speak of their experiences, so that I am persuaded that the schools I attended were fairly representative. And there is every reason

to believe conditions are worse today than they were in the
1940s.

When children hear others of their own age use swear words,
the effect is at once harmful. Even adults have experienced that
when they repeatedly hear profanity the curse words at last have
a tendency to surface in their own thoughts. Soon after I had
started to schools, I began repeating some of the words I had
heard there to the younger children at home. I was innocent as
to their meaning. My parents were so aghast at the words I
was saying, they promptly washed out my mouth with soap and
water.

Similar to profanity are the four-letter words and sex talk
of even the youngest children. I remember how shocked and
surprised I was the first time I heard a fellow first-grader explain
the mysteries of life. I admit his understanding was limited,
but so was mine! Throughout the school years, I overheard
all kinds of filthy talk that had been picked up from the very
gutters of human lust. In the older grades, my classmates were
no longer content to talk about the subject; they began to
experiment.

I can only say in conclusion that the environment in which
I spent my school years, and the immorality of my classmates,
were far removed from the ideal of Christian conduct and
behavior.

We are taking dangerous chances if we expect our children
to mix with the world and not be harmed by it. The Bible
says, "Evil communications corrupt good manners."

Again we quote Menno Simons:

> Beloved brethren in Christ, if you rightly know God
> and His Word, and believe that the end of the righteous is
> everlasting life, and the end of the wicked eternal death,
> then study to the utmost of your power to lead your
> children on the way of life, and to keep them from the
> way of death, as much as in you is. Pray to Almighty God
> for the gift of His grace, that in His great mercy He may
> lead and keep them in the straight path, . . . leading them
> by His Holy Spirit. Watch over their salvation as over

your own souls. Teach them and instruct them, admonish
them, threaten, correct and chastize them, as circumstances
require. Keep them away from good-for-nothing children,
from whom they hear and learn nothing but lying, cursing,
swearing, fighting, and mischief. Direct them to reading
and writing. Teach them to spin and other handicrafts
suitable, useful, and proper to their years and persons. [13]

A hundred years ago there was not such a great difference
in the dress and home environments of true Christians and the
unconverted. Today the gap between them has widened as the
social life of the masses underwent a twentieth-century revolution.
Increased wealth brought materialism, the automobile brought
mobility, and the twin evils of radio and television brought the
sin of the world into the living room. Population increases have
brought larger cities and more crowded communities.

As a result of these changes, we find crime rates going up,
moral standards coming down, and family life falling apart.
The modern child lives in a different world from the children
of our plain groups. How long can we keep this separation,
this distinction, under the pressure of society to make us conform
to its standards? Is it possible if we continue to select that
society's children as companions for our children?

Thirty-five years ago a Mennonite doctor said, "When I
think of a boy going to high school in our present time and
sitting down in a seat alongside a girl who has a skirt away above
her knees and her legs bare, I say, 'God help that boy!' " [14]

What is wrong with public schools? The public schools
present a secular view of life rather than a sacred view. State
schools have always prepared the child for his life on earth,
and were never intended to prepare him for eternity. For the
world, education is training the mind for success in this life.
For the Christian, education is training the child to live for others,
to use his talents in service to God and man, to live an upright
and obedient life, and to prepare for the life to come.

Secular education places too high a value on earthly
riches and attainments. The Bible says to seek first the kingdom

of God and its righteousness. This the public schools
understandably do not do.

C. C. Morrison, former editor of *The Christian Century*,
said in an editorial, "Public education without religion creates a
secular mentality faster than the church can Christianize it."

Public education, in the first place, was acceptable to the
masses of this country only because educators promised that
morality and religion would be upheld. For this reason, public
schools in the past started the day with a devotional period,
and in other ways formally acknowledged God. In the last few
years even this has been outlawed, thus removing the only crutch
some Christians have long used to support their lame excuses.

It appears that in the future there will be less and less
religion in public schools, and if there is any at all, it will be
taught as a subject, a method which is infinitely more harmful
than no teaching at all.

Instead of loyalty to God, the pupil in our state schools
is taught patriotism above all else. The Bible teaches that we
should obey, respect, and pray for the "powers that be," but in
some instances, we must obey God rather than men. The secular
view is to kill the enemy and bomb his cities. The sacred view
is to "resist not evil," but "do good to them that hate you,
and pray for them which despitefully use you, and persecute you."
Which view do we want taught to our children?

A Mennonite minister has this to say:

> For many decades, and especially in modern times,
> our state schools have been accustomed to emphasize
> patriotic ideals, with patriotic songs and programs, along
> with compulsory flag salutes. Many Christian children under
> such influences unconsciously imbibe the sense of the
> superiority of the state as the controlling authority in
> their lives.
>
> The question may be raised as to why it was that
> more than half of our young men during World War II
> took army service instead of remaining true to the
> principle of nonresistance. While not all of this can be
> attributed to their former school life, doubtless the secular

culture of both home and school, along with the patriotic ideas received while in school, contributed to the weak testimony to our professed faith.[15]

In many textbooks, war is portrayed as glory, glamor, and heroism. Just for a sample, read the following paragraph copied from a seventh-grade history, widely used the past ten years in Canada:

> It was on the Savio River that Private Ernest Alvia (Smoky) Smith won his V.C. (Victoria Cross). It is an amazing story.
>
> Smoky's company had managed to cross the Savio and was arranging its defences when it was set upon by three Panther tanks and a platoon of Germans with two guns. Smith coolly let one of the tanks come almost up to him before he fired his Piat gun and put it out of action. Ten Germans jumped off the tank and attacked him. Smoky then moved out into the middle of the road and let them have it with his tommy gun. He shot four and the others fled. Another tank and more soldiers closed in on him, but he stood over a wounded comrade and fought them until they retired. He got the V.C. for that fight, and few great honors have been more boldly won.[16]

Or, for just plain nonsense, venture a glance at a song selected by the Ontario Department of Education for the seventh and eighth grades:

> There was a lady loved a swine,
>   Honey, said she;
> Lovely hog, wilt thou be mine?
>   Oink, said he.
> O tell me, wilt thou have me now,
>   Honey, said she;
> Answer, or my heart will break.
>   Oink, said he.[17]

Do we desire better things for our children than this? I am convinced we do.

What is wrong with public schools? Evolutionism, atheism, and a host of other godless "isms" are not kept out of public schools.

There are many false teachings abroad today. It is a known fact that their supporters make a direct attack upon the schools of the nation because they know this is a fruitful field.

Perhaps the best known and one of the most dangerous of all teachings is the theory of evolution, which denies a Creator God, and maintains that our wonderful and complex world of nature evolved itself.

The theory at its best is ridiculous, and it is hard to understand how it is so widely accepted. Yet humans will believe anything, providing it is the popular thing to do. Surely, God sends them "strong delusion, that they should believe a lie" (2 Thess. 2:8-12).

Edwin Conklin, the biologist, once said, "The probability of life originating from accident is comparable to the probability of the unabridged dictionary resulting from an explosion in a printing shop." When one really considers what life and matter are, even Conklin's words seem like an understatement. Furthermore, someone would have to build the printing shop in the first place.

Another writer has said, "There is no doubt about it that the doctrine of evolution is the greatest curse in our educational system" (Brig. Gen. F. D. Frost). And he was speaking only indirectly of its relationship to Christianity. What he had in mind was what Professor James Bale of Harding College has said, "The materialistic theory of evolution tends to break down moral law and order, and to give free course to the worst passions of men." It is a historical fact that evolution has largely been the inspiration of communism.

In an address before the Mennonite General Conference, August 29, 1929, Dr. C. D. Esch had the following to say:

> I want to say right here, one of the most "damnable heresies" the devil has ever concocted in the pits of hell and is handing out to our boys and girls in our schools and

colleges, is when teachers and authors are trying to lead them to believe that man came from the lower creation, that he is only a "development." It is bad enough physically and spiritually, but do you know that there are books that our boys and girls from the fifth grade on in some states have to read that try to make out that a man sexually is on the same basis as an animal. . . ?

The normal human being, as God expected him to be, is one who is able to control his whole life by the help of his reason and the help of an all powerful God who said, "I will sustain you and underneath are the everlasting arms." So man does not belong to the brute kingdom, and you, fathers and mothers, who have children going to school in the third and fourth, and even in the second grades, examine their textbooks and see what is being taught there— and don't be still about it.[18]

The very doctrine referred to above by Dr. Esch is the one widely proclaimed by John Dewey (1859-1952), the leading figure in the Progressive Education movement. Robert R. Rusk, in *The Doctrines of the Great Educators*, writes of Dewey,

He recognizes no difference between the protozoan and the creature who has been made a little lower than the angels; he refuses to acknowledge another dimension of experience in man than that assigned to animals; culture, art, morality, and religion are all explicable on biological principles.[19]

These are the things that result from the theory of evolution. Evolutionists themselves openly admit their theory can be accepted only by faith. It cannot be proved. And yet we find evolution boldly presented in many textbooks, always as if facts were being given. Even in the younger elementary grades, there are traces of evolutionist teaching. We find it most often in history and science texts, but it crops up in the most unexpected places in many of the other subjects.

Only by concerned and informed Christian teachers can this

evil be combated. It is a matter that confronts most children sooner or later, and if it is then explained, it usually presents no problem. It is in public schools where it may be strongly promoted that this theory is particularly dangerous. This is one more reason for having church schools.

I would like to quote several paragraphs from an editorial in *The Blackboard Bulletin* of May 1963:

> Even though modern-day ministers try to smear over the differences, and to explain Christianity and evolution in the light of each other, there are no greater opposites in the world today. Christianity teaches of a God and Creator. Evolution says there is neither. Christianity teaches the fall of man, and through the cross of Christ, his redemption. Evolution says life is ever more perfect, man is his own savior, controls his own destiny, and has a glorious future. Christianity teaches an "other-cheek" philosophy, love for all mankind. Evolution teaches little more than the law of the jungle, the strong over the weak, militarism, might is right, survival of the fittest. Christianity teaches immortality, and a hope of heaven for the righteous. Evolution says man is only a higher animal, and the grave his end.
>
> Which has the most to offer? Take your choice. There can be no reconciliation between the two. [20]

And when you decide between a church school for your children, or a public school education, you may be making that choice.

Closely allied to the theory of evolution are the activities of the Junior Atheist League, a society that works mainly on the high school and college level. From their own literature we quote the following:

> The League will remove boys and girls from the evil influence of the clergy. It will encourage them to protest against Bible reading and religious worship in public schools.... The attainment of happiness in this world

rather than an eternal bliss in a world to come shall be
taught the rising generation as the chief end of man.
Dispelling the illusions of immortality, the League will free
our sons and daughters from the fear of hell and the hope
of heaven.[21]

We must remember that the Supreme Court decision of
June 17, 1963, in which reciting of the Lord's Prayer in the
opening exercises of a public school was declared unconstitutional,
was largely the work of atheists. The Junior Atheist League,
and its parent society, the American Association for the
Advancement of Atheism, have been sponsoring many of the
recent court cases. They have been working for many years to
abolish God from national life. At last it appears they are getting
results.

The question confronting us is, "What shall we do in the
light of these developments?" The Supreme Court decision
sharply underlines one fact: public schools are rapidly coming
under the rule of the state and federal governments. Soon the
controlling voice will no longer be the local board. Texts and
teachers and curriculums are being standardized from one end of
the land to the other. Standardized procedures turn out a
standardized product—a child who has been formed in the mold
of the modern way of life, and knows nothing of God. "With the
Bible out of the public school system, and evolution and other
anti-scriptural heresies in them, need we wonder at the alarming
increase of unbelief?" [22]

Indeed, too many people in our world today are not as
interested in freedom *of* religion as they are in freedom *from*
religion.

Along with atheism and evolution, several other dangers are
more common in public schools than in our own church schools.

One of these is pornography, obscene photos of nude men
and women in every act of lewdness. A report of the tremendous
increase of this filth was given in the March 1959 *Reader's Digest*,
in an article entitled, "Help Stamp Out This Vile Traffic."
The U.S. Post Office Department reports that organized publishing
and selling of pornography reached a then peak value of half a

million dollars for the year 1958. Three-fourths of this was aimed at, and was reaching, school-age children from ages eleven and up through high school.

According to the article, "These pictures are pure deadly poison. Naked men and girls, singly and commingled, pose wantonly.... The obscenity portrayed strikes an adult mind with an almost physical nauseating shock. The effect upon the unformed mind of a child must be beyond description."

This filth is only one indication of the immorality in the world today. The following appeared in a national magazine some years ago:

> Asking an engineer armed with a dipper to stop the flow of water over Niagara Falls is child's play compared to the teacher's job of combating the flood of misrepresentation, propaganda, and immorality flowing out of Hollywood, book publishing houses, popular magazines, newspapers, radios, and television.[23]

We agree. The job is too big for a teacher. It is the responsibility of the church and the family. Has it been in the best interests of the church over the past one hundred years to have turned this responsibility over to those outside the church? Will it advance our spiritual growth to continue sending large numbers of our children to state schools?

These are questions that we face, as we consider the trends of the times. What are our answers?

What is wrong with public schools? The teachers in the public schools are not of our faith. True, there are sincere and dedicated teachers in the public schools, many of them. They may even be sympathetic to our beliefs, and respect us enough not to teach our children anything against our wishes. We can be thankful for such teachers.

But wait! If an occasion demanded that we leave our homes for a year, and we were unable to take our children along, whom would we choose to oversee them while we were gone? Would we ask the teachers already caring for them half the time to take on full duties as temporary parents? Or would we ask a trusted brother and sister of our faith to take our children into their home?

Do you see the inconsistency of having a teacher who is not of our faith? No matter how sympathetic, such a teacher can come only half way. He can desist from teaching objectionable material, but he is not in a position to teach the desirable material in which our children should be instructed, as long as he himself refuses it by his example.

A few of our church schools employ non-Amish teachers. That is their business, but it would seem they are losing half the benefit of parochial schools. Is it actually necessary to go outside our own church for someone to train up our children in the way they should go?

Some people feel it does not work to have our own teachers, for "familiarity breeds contempt." It is true there is a tendency for children to have less respect for someone they know well. Just the fact that a teacher is Amish makes some children think he does not merit the respect another teacher would.

We do well to recognize this danger and seek to overcome it. Several hundred Amish men and women have taught successfully, proving that it is a problem that can be overcome. We show weak reasoning and a weaker faith if we decide teachers of another faith, or perhaps of no faith at all, would be superior to our own church members, just because of this element of familiarity. If this were not so, what have we been doing all these years by ordaining ministers from our own brotherhood?

What is wrong with public schools? Public schools are changing fast, and we fear not for the better. These changes are in the areas of control, teaching of religion, and subject matter.

Public schools are fast changing control. The days of the one-room school and its district school board are mostly past. The move to consolidated school areas began a number of years ago, and in the United States is in its final stages. This trend toward centralization is not restricted to schools. It is found in churches, industry, and government, so that the average individual has less and less to say that matters.

What does it mean, and what will it lead to?

The creeping evil of socialism, or increasing government

control of almost every area of our lives, can mean only one thing,
the gradual loss of our freedom. Already we have government
plans forced upon us in the form of Social Security, workmen's
compensation insurance, hospitalization and Medicare plans,
farm quotas and soil banks, artificial price controls and subsidies.
As local groups lose control of our schools, we can expect the
government to dictate what will be taught and how.

Did you know that in Russia today many of the children
are raised and trained by the state from the age of two months
on? According to a newspaper report from a Moscow columnist,
this is true. We quote:

> In order to care for the children of all its working
> mothers, Russia has gone into the baby business in a big way.
> Collective baby-raising, it's called, and the U.S.S.R. is a
> world leader in this field. Child care experts and nursery
> school workers from all over the world travel here to
> see the state's mass program for the scientific raising of
> children, according to Marxist-Leninist doctrine.
>
> "We know what's better for the children than their
> mother," I was told by Mrs. Eugenia Radina, chief of
> the laboratory of education of younger children at the
> Academy of Pedagogical Preschool Sciences. "The government
> would like every child, whether the mother is working or
> not, to be given over to the state for scientific care."
>
> The children are taught "love of their country and
> esteem and love for the founder of the Soviet State,
> Vladimir Lenin." A key part of their program includes the
> laying of fresh flowers before the gigantic picture of Lenin,
> which dominates the auditorium of each nursery school.[24]

We will not attempt to predict what may yet come to pass
in our country if present trends continue. But if the Lord tarries,
it will surely mean a continued loss of our liberties, including
freedom of religion. And it may come about so smoothly and
deceptively that we will play into the very hands of the enemies
of the church.

Religion is fast disappearing from public schools. Recent

court cases have even declared religious devotions to be contrary to the U.S. Constitution, which forbids "establishment" of religion.

The Supreme Court ruling of 1963 affected over half of the U.S. schools, especially in the South and East where the majority of schools have always opened the day's program with prayer or Bible readings.

Other court cases have followed the lead. The attorney general of the state of Washington has ruled that commencement services which are religious in nature may not be held in public schools. He also has said the distribution of the Bible in public schools by the Gideons is unconstitutional.

On the other hand, California's attorney general, Stanley Mosk, has ruled that teaching Darwin's theory of evolution in public schools does not violate constitutional guarantees of religious freedom.

The standards and curricula of public schools are changing, too. Fifty years ago a girl in shorts at school would have been promptly expelled. Yet it is a fact that just recently a minister's daughter attending an Akron, Ohio, high school was expelled because she would not wear shorts to gym practice!

We cannot understand why anyone would be forced to take part in gym practice in the first place, though we are told it is a required subject for two years in high school in the state of Ohio.

Similarly, we read the following in the physical education program of the Ontario Department of Education:

Dance for Primary Children, Gr. 1-3
Young children are naturally spontaneous and imaginative. These characteristics are fostered through art, music, and drama. Movement is another outlet through which children can express their ideas and moods. In the expression of these ideas and moods through movement, movement becomes dance. . . .

The children will find their movement less restricted if arrangements can be made to have them work in shorts, T-shirts, and their bare feet.

These are examples of the importance that is attached to extra activities in the public schools. Sports, music, plays, and other entertainment take a large cut of money and time. Dancing lessons are a part of the program in many schools.

A Pennsylvania mother has written of her experiences:

> Our two older children graduated from public school. During their school years, particularly in the upper grades, they specialized in extracurricular activities. To them school meant a good time and social life. Studies were got through with as little time and effort as possible to maintain passing grades. The school enjoyed a reputation in sports and music, and encouragement was given along these lines, even at the expense of scholastic attainment.[25]

The sailing of Sputnik through the skies in 1957 marked a turning point for many schools. In the United States, the public became alarmed at how fast Russia was gaining in the space race. Pressure was at once put on the public schools of the nation. The American pupil had dillydallied around long enough. It was time to start studying.

The result has been a reslanting of textbooks and a stepped-up program in science and mathematics. But very few of the "pleasures" of school life have been removed. This has resulted in armloads of books lugged home for evening homework, while extra activities continue to take part of the day.

The public schools are not striving for the same goal Christian parents are. We are not interested in building missiles and jet aircraft. They are not interested in building Christians. We must go separate ways.

3

Showdown at an Amish Schoolhouse
Donald A. Erickson

Donald A. Erickson is a professor of education at the University of Chicago. He has written extensively on Amish school problems and edited a book entitled *Public Controls for Nonpublic Schools.*

In "Showdown at an Amish Schoolhouse" Professor Erickson recounts and analyzes the Iowa school controversy. The Iowa case received widespread public attention and illustrates the subtle dilemmas faced by public officials confronted by Amish noncompliance with school statutes.

THE SHOWDOWN

Its engine sputtering against the cold, the school bus left Oelwein, Iowa, for the Old Order Amish settlement a few miles southwest. Aboard were a superintendent of schools, a school nurse, and a driver, all intent on bringing some forty children to a public school, against the wishes of the Amish leaders. The Plain People had been violating the law, staffing their private schools with uncertified teachers. It was 7:45 A.M. on Friday, November 19, 1965.

On the way to the Amish settlement, the bus stopped
momentarily in the tiny hamlet of Hazleton, and Owen Snively,
principal of the Hazleton Elementary School, climbed aboard.
He had been appointed temporary truant officer for the task
at hand, for the Amish had long regarded him as a friend,
and it was to his school that the youngsters were to be brought.
A homespun warmth and candor about him reflected boyhood
years on an Iowa farm. In his love of the land and the outdoors,
he had much in common with the Plain People. But he was
apprehensive concerning the events that lay ahead.

The superintendent, Arthur Sensor, counted seventeen
carloads of newsmen and sightseers, waiting outside the school
for the drama to begin. "If I'd had any sense," he says, "I'd have
gone back home the moment I saw those cars." Sensor had avoided
action against the Amish for most of his thirty-eight months in
office, for he was fond of many of the Plain People, and he knew
where national sentiments lay in this regard.

With one exception (Abe Yoder had his driveway blocked
so the bus could not enter), the delegation called at the homes
of all the Amish who had been breaking the school code,
occasionally stepping inside to talk. At each stop, Truant Officer
Snively declared that he had come to take the children to the
Hazleton school, under the authority of Iowa's truancy statute.
Many of the parents, knowing what was planned, had hid their
young in the fields ahead of time. Though Christ Raber reported
his offspring were "not here," the driver claimed to see them
peeking through a doorway. William Schmucker's children were
present when the bus arrived, but he would not willingly let
them leave the premises. Still hoping to avoid trouble, the group
moved on from farm to farm, emptyhanded. After the last home
had been visited, the bus turned back down the gravel road to
Amish School No. 1 (also known as the "South School"),
where many of the pupils had already arrived for their studies.
By the time instruction was scheduled to begin, the sheriff,
deputy sheriff, and county attorney appeared on the scene,
along with numerous fathers and mothers.

Entering the building, Snively explained that it was legally
necessary to transport the pupils to the school in town. He said

he was their friend, wanting only to help them, and promised a warm welcome in Hazleton. Now, he asked, would they be good children and quietly file into the bus behind Sheriff Fred Beier. The sheriff started slowly toward the bus, the boys and girls following in an orderly single file. Suddenly, when most of the youngsters were outside, either the teacher or one of the mothers shouted in German, "Run!" The pupils bolted for the field at the rear of the schoolyard, scrambled through the barbed-wire fence, and ran through the adjoining cornfield into the woods beyond. Some never stopped running until they reached their homes. Wisely, the officials declined to give chase. Emanuel Borntreger, a portly boy of thirteen, could not keep up with his peers, waddled confusedly into the deputy sheriff's arms, and was led weeping to the bus. Sara Schmucker, a tiny six-year-old, was left behind in the cornfield, shivering and screaming distractedly. Tears coursing down his own face, Superintendent Sensor took her to the sheriff's heated automobile and tried to calm her.

On the lookout for interesting pictures, a newsman told Truant Officer Snively, "Some kids are hiding in the classroom. You can see them through the window." Peering through the pane on tiptoe, Snively provided a scene that appeared in papers across the nation the next day, along with photographs of children hightailing for the corn; a doe-like girl with stricken eyes, fleeing in blind panic while looking over her shoulder; Teacher Katie Miller, wiping her cheeks while her charges disappeared; Emanuel Borntreger, whimpering in the grasp of two husky officers; and the county attorney, stalking along the fence as if in search of some vanished quarry.

When no other pupils could be found, the men left Sara and Emanuel in the schoolhouse, urged the Amish to return the children to their studies at once (it was bitter cold), and announced that no further interruptions would occur that day. On the way back to Hazleton, however, Snively suggested that "since the Hookies pulled a fast one on us, we should pull a fast one on them." (The Amish, who fasten their clothing with hooks and eyes because of a taboo on ornaments, are often called "Hooks" or "Hookies." The non-Amish nearby are frequently

referred to as "Buttons" or "English.") During the noon hour,
Sensor and the sheriff suddenly appeared at Amish School No. 1
("South School"), and Snively and the deputy sheriff at Amish
School No. 2 (also known as "North School" or "Charity Flats
School"). Soon the bus followed, first to one school and then to
the other, and the pupils were carefully loaded aboard, one at a
time, and whisked to Hazleton. No parents or newsmen were
present, and the youngsters offered no resistance.

At Hazleton, preappointed pupil hosts met the bus, welcomed
the Old Order children, and escorted them to classrooms,
helping to settle them and provide them with books. During the
afternoon, the newcomers took part in studies, played games
with their classmates, and were treated to cookies and milk.
Many of the Amish youngsters viewed the whole affair as high
adventure and sang and joked all the way home. But some were
emotionally shaken as a result of being forced to disobey their
parents. According to reports, a few were punished for going
too enthusiastically to Hazleton.

The Plain People assumed that on Monday the authorities
would arrive via the same route as on Friday, calling first at
South School; so the most important Amish leaders and their
attorney, William Sindlinger, were posted there. Instead, the
entourage entered the community from the north. As before,
the officials went first to several homes along the way, and most
of the youngsters had fled. Abner Schwartz's children darted
for the cornfield just as the bus turned in at the gate, but
Truant Officer Snively was agile enough to retrieve them. Mrs.
Schwartz dropped to her knees in tears, pleading with the men
to leave her little ones alone. Her husband angrily kicked a
milk pail all over the barnyard. Superintendent Sensor refused
to let the children leave the bus, but assured Mrs. Schwartz
they would come to no harm. She then asked to be allowed to
come with them to the school, and when Sensor assented,
climbed inside.

At the North School, a large horse-drawn wagon sat astride
the driveway, blocking passage, and the Amish attorney's colleague,
Wallace Read, stood nearby, reading aloud from a document.
Anyone but Truant Officer Snively would be liable for trespass,

Read intoned, upon entering these private grounds. Snively huffed that he was entitled to bring assistants. Sheriff Beier said he had responsibility to take action wherever the laws were broken in rural Buchanan County, and he proceeded to move the team and wagon, permitting the bus to enter.

Mrs. Schwartz and her frightened brood scurried into the schoolhouse. The entry-room was full of weeping women. A group of stern-faced fathers stood outside, guarding the door. Truant Officer Snively pushed his way through the men (the Plain People are pacifists), and brushed off the mothers who pulled at his clothing and begged him not to proceed. Sheriff Beier followed soon after. As Snively stepped inside, the pupils began singing, half-hysterically, chorus after chorus of "Jesus Loves Me," led by a teacher who circled the room in agitation. Soon mothers entered to embrace their children protectively. Snively attempted to pry a screaming schoolboy loose from a desk. A group of girls ran into a corner to huddle and sob as Snively approached them. Fathers burst in to protest. County Attorney Lemon shouted his disgust at the way the Amish were behaving. Newsmen came in, scribbling madly. Children wailed, women whimpered, flashbulbs popped, and tides of emotion swept the room. More than sixteen months later, the officials still show their embarrassment when asked about this event.

Retreating outdoors, Superintendent Sensor, Sheriff Beier, and County Attorney Lemon decided to fly to Des Moines for assistance. By 11 A.M. that same morning, the three men were airborne for the capital. Themselves upset, they left behind them an Old Order community in a state of shock. Some children could not be composed for the rest of the day.

As news of the showdown spread, citizens in the area sprang to the defense of their representatives. Strong support was soon expressed by the Oelwein *Daily Register*, the Rotary Club, and the Chamber of Commerce. Two statewide organizations, the Iowa State Education Association and the Iowa Association of School Administrators, applauded the "firm position" that had been taken. But in general, an opposite trend appeared outside the immediate vicinity. Hostile phone calls, telegrams, and mail poured in from all parts of the continent. Many commentators blistered Sensor, Snively, and their colleagues in the nation's news media. In Cedar Rapids, some eighty miles away, WMT-TV had supported Oelwein's leaders up to this point. Now it condemned what it called "legalized kidnapping":

> Force had been used on the Amish before, but always on the Amish parents who were guilty of violating the law. Now, force has been used against the Amish children, who are guilty of nothing. They have done their parents' bidding as good children do; and as a reward, they have been frightened, man-handled, and forced to violate their religious convictions. . . . Mr. Lemon [the county attorney] and school officials have acted most unwisely. Their ultimate weapon has turned public opinion sharply against them, as ultimate weapons always do. . . . Whatever the final outcome of this distasteful controversy, we urgently suggest that any future prosecution of the Amish be directed only against the guilty. Leave the innocent children alone.

The confrontation was obviously harmful to the Amish youngsters, damaging to Iowa's public image, and destructive of trust between the Plain People and local authorities. What circumstances can explain such hostilities between a gentle farming folk and apparently well-intentioned public officials?

THE CAUSE CÉLÈBRE

There is an obvious linkage between the showdown with the Amish and an informal agreement in the fall of 1961. Until that time, the Hazleton and Oelwein public schools were located in separate districts. It had been suggested for years that the two districts merge and all high school students be educated in Oelwein, for Hazleton High was too small to offer adequate programs. The proposal was supported by numerous Hazletonians, especially those who wanted to give their young a strong preparation preparation for college. A few families were paying tuition and providing their own transportation to send their offspring to high school in Oelwein.

But many Hazletonians opposed reorganization, remembering years of rivalry between the two towns and thinking that the loss of high school and school board headquarters would seriously weaken their community. Many felt the proposed merger was tantamount to a take-over by the city of Oelwein, which had threatened for years to eclipse its tiny neighbor five miles south. Some Hazleton people still complain that the Oelwein *Daily Register* trumpets the escapades of Hazleton teen-agers and ignores similar high jinks at home. In Oelwein, where nothing was to be lost through reorganization, sentiments were strong for approval. There, the school district would be enlarged, the high school program broadened, the tax base improved.

The Hazleton school board unanimously fought the projected merger and refused to put the matter before the voters. Residents who desired the alliance with Oelwein then formed a committee and, abetted by Oelwein school officials, filed enough petitions to require a referendum, scheduled for November 8, 1961. Issues of school district reorganization are often severely contested in rural America, but the Hazleton-Oelwein fracas grew unusually bitter. Those who supported the proposal were described as "for Oelwein"; those who damned it, "for Hazleton." Old friends stopped talking. Secret meetings were held. Vicious rumors spread. Each faction accused the other of lies and distortions. On both sides a few hotheads who normally lacked an audience found attentive ears.

As for the Plain People, they petitioned a joint meeting of the Buchanan, Fayette, and Bremer County school boards, which was to draw the boundaries of the new district, asking to be excluded from the jurisdiction of Oelwein officials. (In Iowa and several other states outside the South, the county level of school government is intermediate between the state and the operating districts. Generally overlying several local school districts, the county unit provides services that small districts would have difficulty maintaining by themselves.) The Amish wanted to be attached to the adjoining Fairbank Township area, where one-room public schools were still maintained for Old Order pupils. Hazleton's two Amish schools were themselves once public. But when the Hazleton Consolidated School District was formed,

back in 1947, farm boys and girls were transferred to the
consolidated school in town, and the Plain People, unwilling to
have their young educated in environs they saw as hostile,
bought the abandoned one-room schoolhouses and "went private."
Where farm children attend nonpublic schools, income from
school taxes on their parents' land is 99 and 44/100 per cent
gravy for the public school districts. Even when rural pupils
attend simple one-room public schools, the potential tax income
from the area often exceeds the school expenditures. Coveting
these resources, Oelwein officials helped arrange the rejection of
the Plain People's request to be "set out."

At the time in question, Sensor's predecessor, A. A. Kaskadden, was still superintendent of the Oelwein public
schools. "Kas" is described by those who knew him as brilliant,
expert in virtually every aspect of school affairs. But he was
nervous, anxious, and full of self-doubt. He drove himself
mercilessly and worried about everything. Kaskadden was
distraught about prospects for the reorganization referendum.
He knew Oelwein citizens would support the merger
overwhelmingly, but the approval of the voters in both districts
was required. Hazletonians, he thought, would split fifty-fifty
on the issue, and the Amish, perturbed because they were not
permitted to stay out of the proposed new district, might
sabotage his efforts by casting their ballots negatively.

In September 1961, Kas wrote Paul Johnston, State
Superintendent of Public Instruction, asking for help in putting
the referendum across. A little later the two men conferred at
a meeting of professional educators. Johnston was known in
Iowa as "an apostle of school district reorganization." He had
already attempted to influence Hazleton voters by announcing
that state approval of their high school would be withdrawn after
July 1, 1962, the date on which the projected reorganization
was to take effect. Johnston suggested that Kaskadden win the
Amish vote by promising to revert to a practice still followed in
nearby school districts, maintaining simple one-room public schools
in Amish communities. The new board, Johnston suggested,
could reincorporate Hazleton's two Old Order schools into the
public school system by leasing the buildings for a nominal fee,

could provide two certified teachers at public expense, and could adapt the programs to the convictions of the Amish leaders. The fiscal advantages for the Plain People would be considerable, and they would lose practically nothing in the process.

But Johnston had fought for the elimination of one-room schools in Iowa! "If we are caught maintaining one-room schools for the Amish," Kaskadden demanded, "what will happen to our state approval?" Johnston replied that the State Department of Education, knowing the particulars of the situation, would raise no embarrassing questions. Kaskadden predicted that the Amish would vote for reorganization if such a compact were arranged, but he insisted he would take no steps in that direction unless Johnston sanctioned the strategy in writing, promising in a letter that the status of the Oelwein schools would not be jeopardized. Back in Oelwein, Kaskadden confided to his board members, "Johnston will never write that letter!" A few days later, the following communication arrived:

October 12, 1961

Mr. A. A. Kaskadden
Oelwein Public School
Oelwein, Iowa

Dear Mr. Kaskadden:

I am in receipt of your letter concerning your reorganization and I am sorry that you have not been able to get in touch with me before this.

I recall our conversation concerning the Amish settlement located in the Hazleton Consolidated School District. I am glad to set forth in this letter my views concerning the situation as it exists.

I think that because of the situation as it exists and the feelings of the Amish people that the Board would, and should, recognize that they have to give consideration to the people making up the new district. As I suggested when we were visiting, I would recommend that if the reorganization took place that the Board hire teachers and provide supervision for the two schools which the Amish

people are now operating. I think the new Board should
provide good facilities and equipment, and good teachers
for these schools but in so doing recognize these people's
feeling concerning education.

I think this would be a good solution for these people
and also I think your board and the future Board should
undertake to understand their beliefs and work with them
in giving their children the basic education that they
firmly believe in. We would, I am sure, raise no questions
concerning this arrangement so long as the facilities were
adequate and well qualified teachers furnished to teach
these children along with the type of instruction materials
that I am sure your Board would insist upon providing.
We would not adversely judge your school because of this
as we do have an understanding of the situation.

Trusting this gives you the information you requested,
I remain

Sincerely yours,

(signed)

Paul F. Johnston
State Superintendent of
Public Instruction

Kaskadden wasted no time at this point. He held several
discussions with Dan Borntreger, venerable chairman of the Amish
School Committee, bringing copies of Paul Johnston's statement.
Gentle in mien but renowned for his shrewdness, with aquiline
profile, white beard, and silken hair around a bald pate,
Borntreger is well cast as biblical patriarch. He was not easily
persuaded that Kas and the board could make a lasting covenant,
for he knew that they had no legal authority to bind the board
that would be elected after reorganization. "I expect to be
superintendent for many years to come," Kaskadden said, "and I
will always recommend that the board honor our arrangement."
At least one board member talked with Borntreger; the member
said he had every anticipation of being reelected, and he, too,
would keep faith. Buck Kjar, chairman of the Hazleton
reorganization committee, urged the Amish to place confidence

in the promises of Kas and his colleagues. Finally convinced, Borntreger set about to persuade his confreres to vote for reorganization. C. J. Arthaud, then president of the Hazleton school board, tells of spending several hours with Kaskadden at this juncture, trying unsuccessfully to persuade him not to bargain for the Plain People's ballots.

Just four days before the referendum, Johnston's letter was published in full in the Oelwein *Daily Register*, which thirty-two Amishmen were receiving at the time. In the same issue, a letter to the editor complained that "the Oelwein Community School District has promised the Amish people tax paid schools for their children. . . . It looks to these writers that someone is buying votes." In addition, the Oelwein board inserted a statement of its own:

> Should this reorganization proposal pass on November 8th and the newly elected board of education see fit to concur in Mr. Johnston's recommendation and again take over the operation of the rural schools in the Amish area, the same curriculum, the same standards, and the same quality of teachers would be used as in all other schools of the district.
>
> . . . To transport these children to Hazleton at taxpayers [sic] expense would probably cost as much as to educate them in the rural schools as the Amish desire.
>
> The present Oelwein Board of Education feels that the desires of all minority groups should be given full consideration whenever possible providing these desires are legal and lead to better education. . . .
>
> The Oelwein Board of Education could not legally and did not make a definite commitment to the Amish people. We simply passed on the recommendations given us by the State Department of Public Instruction that legally the newly elected board of education for the new district if reorganization passed, could and should give consideration to the Amish peoples' request that their schools be operated under the full jurisdiction of the duly elected board of education.

On November 8, 1961, citizens in the Oelwein school district approved reorganization overwhelmingly (993 to 231), while in Hazleton, with 44 Amishmen voting, the measure passed by a margin of only 49 (264 to 215). Assuming that the Plain People supported reorganization, in accordance with the agreement, it is obvious that they could have defeated the measure by voting negatively. But Dan Borntreger and the Oelwein school officials had underestimated the reaction that would follow. Hazletonians who had opposed reorganization were furious concerning the behind-the-scenes compact and the Amish role in the election. Key Hazletonians to this day insist that the followers of the Old Order "swung the election and forced us to come under the Oelwein board." Residents who wanted the referendum to pass had brought several carloads of Amishmen to town to cast ballots. Seeing the Amish at the polls, numerous local people were so incensed they left without voting, and others angrily stayed home as the news spread. The resentment was exacerbated when, in March, 1962, not one member of the Hazleton board was elected to represent the new district, while Buck Kjar, who headed the despised Hazleton reorganization committee, was placed in office with all five members of the old Oelwein board. Ancient grievances against the Plain People were revived. Hazleton citizens vowed to take stern steps against any Hook caught breaking the law. Intense pressures were exerted to prevent the new school board from taking over the two Old Order schools in accordance with the agreement, and a close watch was kept to determine "whether Oelwein will make the Amish obey the school code the way Hazleton always did."

By this time, it appears, many Hazletonians had developed what a former Oelwein school board member describes as "very deep, bitter prejudice" against the Amish, comparable, he avers, to attitudes toward Negroes in Selma, Alabama. Local leaders confess they cannot quite understand how these antagonisms arose, except that the circumstances of the referendum played an important part.

The Plain People are the object of some criticism wherever they are found. Their nonconformity is itself a mild insult to the larger society. Generally preferring to limit contacts with Buttons, the denizens of the Old Order sometimes seem cliquish and unfriendly. On occasion their refusal to retaliate when attacked is viewed as cowardice. In a number of areas, the existence of many Amish conscientious objectors meant that a disproportionate number of "English" were sent to battle during World War II, for a county-by-county quota system was in force. Forbidden to possess radios, television sets, automobiles, plumbing, washing machines, refrigerators, sofas, sports equipment, and "fancy" clothing, they put little money into local purchases and much into land and ironware crocks. Yet they frequently ride in their neighbors' cars and ask to use their neighbors' telephones. Since each church district is autonomous, some bishops permit what others prohibit. Even within a single community, what is allowed at one time may be forbidden at another. Now and then the Amish are exempted from legislation concerning schools and social security, and a few Buttons object to this "unfairness." But in most areas, the Amish are admired, in spite of these foibles and inconsistencies, for they are usually skillful farmers, industrious, self-reliant, and honest, They never leave a brother in need.

Around Hazleton, however, they are subject to a dismal list of charges, often exaggerated, unsupported, or inconsistent. Two or three Legionnaires were fiercely offended by a juvenile prank in Amish School No. 1 that left the American flag on the floor, and by doodlings, interpreted as disrespectful, found in some civics workbooks. A few residents who lost sons in the war still act as if the Plain People were entirely to blame. When a member of the Old Order recently bought up a deceased friend's mortgage, apparently to protect the widow from an "English" creditor, this was evidence to local people, strangely, that "the Hooks want to be in a position to coerce each other financially." As sociologists and anthropologists recognize, many issues that are secular in the urbanized world are sacred in folk societies. But when Amishmen cite religious principle as the basis for most decisions, Hazleton people accuse them of "using" religion as an excuse for anything they want to do." The Plain People say their community needs isolation to survive; consequently their young must be limited to a simple elementary education in

rural schools. Scholars who have studied the culture agree. But
locally the Amish are branded as hypocrites, motivated by
economic greed, wanting only to keep their schooling costs down,
and hoping to exploit child labor in the fields. Not all Amish
are honest, of course, but as a people they are acknowledged
by social scientists and most businessmen who serve them to
exhibit unusual integrity. But because a few young blades hide
transistor radios under broad-brimmed hats and buggy seats,
citizens nearby declare the Old Order "makes people deceitful."
Neighbors almost universally aver that the Plain People are happy
and carefree—"perhaps happier than we are." Yet some of the
same individuals describe the Amish community as if it were
a concentration camp—where children are chained to beds, where
barefoot women run farms while their husbands loaf and travel,
where the young are "worked to death," and where aging wives
are allowed to die in childbirth as a substitute for divorce.
The Amish are depicted at some times as so wealthy they
should be ashamed to let sympathizers pay their fines, but at
other times as unsuccessful and poverty stricken ("they don't
use enough fertilizer"), living in dilapidated lean-tos.
Out of a community of at least five hundred, local leaders
identify about fourteen Amishmen who have left the fold in
recent decades, yet argue that the young are deserting in such
alarming numbers the community will soon disintegrate. Defectors
from the subculture are depicted as "getting along beautifully"
in their new surroundings, but their education is condemned
as cutting off all chances of survival in the outside world.
Old Order adolescents are pitied for their drab, iron-clad lives,
yet their purported barnyard orgies are discussed with evangelical
imagination ("They aren't as righteous as they claim to be!").
One board member recently emphasized that modern agriculture
demands a far better schooling than the Plain People receive.
Almost in the next breath, in response to a question, he
described some of the Amish as unsurpassed as farmers.

    The post-referendum animosity in Hazleton could hardly
be ignored in Oelwein. School leaders were particularly sensitive
to voter opinion at the time, for a bond issue referendum to
finance an urgently needed high school addition had recently been

defeated. Now that Hazleton youths would be bussed to Oelwein, the space shortage was especially critical. Hazletonians had been alienated badly enough through the reorganization itself. It seemed that the second bond election, soon to come, would fail if the school board further angered local people by complying with the compact with the Amish. What could Superintendent Kaskadden do?

THE DOUBLE STANDARD

In a communication dated May 7, 1962, the Oelwein school board announced two conditions which, according to the Amish and several board members themselves, had never been mentioned to the Plain People before the reorganization referendum of November 1961. First, if the board took over the two Amish schools, there could be little or no tailoring of the academic program to suit the religious convictions of the parents, even though State Superintendent Johnston's now-famous letter had urged the board to "recognize these people's feeling concerning education" and "undertake to understand their beliefs and work with them in giving their children the basic education that they firmly believe in," and in spite of Kaskadden's repeated assurances to Dan Borntreger. Second, the arrangement must be *temporary*. "It would appear obvious," the board declared, "that Mr. Johnston's letter advising us to work with the Amish people in these schools ... [was intended] to make the transition of these [Amish] pupils to a public school setup easier. Realistically and in all honesty and fairness, it should be pointed out that the ultimate state requirement will demand that these pupils will be incorporated into the school at Hazleton where we have a reasonable chance to have at least one teacher for each elementary grade."

In the Oelwein *Daily Register* for November 4, 1961, four days before the referendum, the board had said: "Should ... the newly elected board ... again take over the operation of the rural schools in the Amish area, the same curriculum, the same standards, and the same quality of teachers would be used as in all other schools of the district." The Amish paid no attention

to this one statement, however, for no such idea had been
brought up in their several conversations with Kaskadden and his
colleagues. It was easy to assume that this isolated utterance,
appearing in the newspaper virtually on the eve of the referendum,
was public relations copy and nothing more, intended to pacify
a few citizens who were complaining about the understanding
with the Plain People. If Kaskadden and the board had wanted
to apprise the Amish of a new condition, stating it in a single
sentence in a small item in the *Register* was the wrong method,
and four days before an election that had involved months of
haggling and planning was the wrong time.

As the Amish see it, the sudden introduction of two
far-reaching provisions represented a deliberate attempt to back
out of the compact, for Kaskadden and the school board knew the
Plain People would never accept such demands. "They wanted to
be able to say that they offered to run our schools but we
wouldn't cooperate," one Amishman declares.

The second blow fell on May 14, just one week later.
In response to inquiries from Kaskadden, State Superintendent
Johnston sent two of his regional consultants to Oelwein,
ostensibly to advise the school board and the Amish concerning
the specific improvements that would have to be made in
Hazleton's Old Order schools before they could be taken over
as public schools. The consultants, Melvin Anderson and Thomas
Green, inspected the two buildings, along with Kaskadden and
several members of his board.

The delegation found the schools primitive, as indeed they
still are. The Amish are committed to the simple life, shorn of
many conveniences the outside world regards as necessities.
In the manner of a bygone era, they know how to maintain
healthful conditions without benefit of plumbing and electricity.
They scorn many modern educational materials and devices,
for they want merely to rear their young to manage farms and
kitchens. But people who have seen only tiled bathrooms
are certain to be shocked by a privy. In contrast to a
chrome-plated faucet, a simple well and pump may seem
unsanitary. It is easy to forget that generations of Americans
learned to read without lightbulbs.

In keeping with the Plain People's philosophy, their schools
are rustic, reflecting little attention to esthetics. The two buildings
near Hazleton are reasonably clean and cheerful, though finished
rather roughly inside and out and marred in spots by flaking
paint. Each is furnished with two outdoor privies, a coal shed,
and a well with a manual pump. The North School boasts two
see-saws, two swings, and some old tires as playground equipment;
the South School has none at all.

In each case the only entrance is through a small vestibule,
with shelves and nails for lunch buckets and coats. Each classroom
has rough board floors, generations-worn; extra tall windows on
two sides for ventilation and light (no electricity); short shelves
holding a potpourri of dog-eared books; home-made cupboards
for construction paper; a kitchen sink with water crock and paper
towel dispenser; a large Regulator clock clucking high on the wall;
bits of blackboard; five rows of ancient desks; a teacher's desk
and chair; a hard bench or two for recitations; two or three
sturdy work tables; cardboard boxes full of discarded textbooks;
and some roll-up maps that should be priceless as antiques.
Heat radiates from a massive stove at the rear, stoked by boys
assigned to the task. Pupils' drawings (virtually all brightly colored
rural scenes) are tacked here and there.

The South School had been closed for the summer (in
violation of the statutes) when the inspection team arrived, but
Amishman Andy Kaufman provided a key. The officials professed
profound shock at what they saw. They had never imagined,
they said, that conditions were so bad, so utterly degrading.
One man stuck his head into a privy, emerged with a grimace,
and commented, "Ugh!" Another protested the presence of a
bird's nest on an exterior window sill. Still others worried about
mud puddles near the well. Virtually no supplementary reading
materials were available. Several texts and workbooks were badly
outdated. In a meeting that very night with the Oelwein board
and two representatives of the Amish community, without
contacting Des Moines for Paul Johnston's approval, the state
department officers suddenly reversed the recommendation
contained in his widely publicized letter of October 12, 1961.
The Amish schools were impossible, Anderson and Green

announced, and could never be brought up to an acceptable standard. The State Department of Education would permit the Oelwein Board to operate these schools *for the first six grades only and for two years at the very most.* Before this could be done, furthermore, the Amish must agree to send all seventh- and eighth-grade pupils to Hazleton at once, with the other children to follow within two years. From that point on, the Oelwein board could say it was powerless to help the Amish unless they agreed to the state department's conditions, which of course the Plain People were unlikely to do.

This dramatic reversal of state department policy is the most puzzling event in the entire controversy over Hazleton's Old Order schools, not only because two men in the field purportedly took it upon themselves to countermand their superior's recommendation without even checking with him, but also because of its blatant incompatibility with state department policy less than twenty miles away. At the time of Anderson and Green's ruling, public school districts just west of the Hazleton district were operating seven one-room schools and one two-room school in the countryside for Amish pupils. State department consultants made regular visits to these districts, but the schools were never condemned, although, as late as March 1967, all eight lacked plumbing, all were served by wells similar to those at Hazleton's Amish schools, two had no electricity, and at least one looked considerably more neglected than the schools pronounced impossible by Anderson and Green. In March 1967, a regional consultant for the state department visited five of these schools (including the two without electricity), now maintained by the Wapsie Valley Community School district, and expressed his delight at the way the district was providing for the education of the Amish.

Until recently, these primitive public schools for Old Order pupils were maintained by small rural districts whose boards were composed mostly or entirely of Amishmen. By July 1966, under a new Iowa law, all public elementary schools were required to belong to districts providing instruction at the secondary level. Many observers predicted that the remaining one- and two-room public schools in Amish settlements would be closed as a result, and that Oelwein's debacle would be duplicated elsewhere as the Plain People established more schools of their own, staffed with uncertified teachers.

Three of the schools in question became part of the Jesup Community School District, southwest of Hazleton, and five joined the Wapsie Valley Community School District to the northwest. But leaders in Jesup and Wapsie Valley cleverly avoided Oelwein's dilemma. The town schools, they argued, would be overcrowded if the Old Order pupils were assigned to them, and to make space for the Amish would entail serious expense. It would be financially necessary, then, to continue operating the primitive schools in Amish neighborhoods, at least for the present. The Jesup district has candidly left the schools for the Plain People much as they were, doing little to alter either physical facilities or academic programs. The teachers, though provisionally certified, have but meager formal qualifications, are paid at a rate considerably below Jesup's salary schedule, and would never be tolerated by the state department, Jesup officials declare, if used in other public schools. Science instruction is omitted in compliance with the wishes of the Amish leaders. In Wapsie Valley, similarly, teachers in the one-room schools for the Amish are remunerated at levels considerably below the regular salary schedule, and the buildings are similar to those maintained by Dan Borntreger's committee. The superintendent has made a special effort to gain the confidence of the Plain People, however, and they have agreed to the addition of courses in science.

Clearly, a double standard has been in force in northeastern Iowa for the past five years. The Oelwein, Jesup, and Wapsie Valley school districts all have benefited fiscally through the annexation of Old Order communities. Oelwein alone argues that it cannot justify the costs of maintaining rural schools for the Amish. By state department edict, furthermore, Hazleton's Amish have been forbidden the very accommodations the department has lauded elsewhere.

In terms of local attitudes, however, the difference in policy between Oelwein and the other two districts is not difficult to explain. Only around Hazleton is hostility toward the Plain People so intense that officials have dared not give the Amish access to simple one-room public schools. But why the conflicting actions of the state department? Perhaps the department innocently blundered into inconsistency, as every large bureaucracy occasionally does. The inconsistency came, however, at the very time when Superintendent Kaskadden needed an excuse to abandon his covenant with the Amish. As a long-standing friend of Kas, State Superintendent Johnston had previously invented a maneuver that helped guarantee passage of the reorganization referendum. Was he now taking Kaskadden off another hook? Could Anderson and Green have come to Oelwein with orders to be surprised and shocked and to reverse Johnston's recommendation accordingly? The theory cannot be proved, but it fits the circumstances well.

But Kaskadden is gone, and leaders in Hazleton and Oelwein seem genuinely unaware of the double standard. The most common explanation for the controversy over Old Order education is that Dan Borntreger and some sixteen families in his group are being unusually stubborn. "All the other Amish in the area are attending public schools, but these Hookies refuse to send their children to Hazleton." However, the Hazleton school is radically different from the schools the other Amish attend— in its physical make-up, in the nature of its surroundings, in its programs and activities, and in the composition of its pupil population. And Borntreger once covenanted with Oelwein officials to obtain schools precisely like those his confreres nearby have patronized.

A few months later, in September 1962, for the first time in history both of Hazleton's Amish schools reopened with Old Order teachers who were equipped with only an eighth-grade education (the Amish generally do not believe in instruction beyond that level). The Plain People have steadfastly refused ever since to employ certified instructors. This comparatively new stance is defended as a matter of religious principle. But do the Amish commandments change, local citizens ask, permitting state-approved tutors for fifteen years and then forbidding them? It is difficult to determine exactly why the Amish suddenly refused to comply with the Iowa law they had obeyed for so long a time. Their leaders were never happy,

it appears, with the certified teachers they imported from outside.
It is widely conceded that Dan Borntreger's group had to pay
a premium to obtain legally recognized instructors and generally
obtained poorly qualified individuals even then, for those who
could obtain positions elsewhere were usually unwilling to work
in such primitive schools. Apparently several of these schoolmarms
lacked initiative, communicated poorly with the pupils, failed to
maintain proper discipline, and reacted defensively to suggestions
from parents and community leaders. It is probably true, as the
Plain People argue, that many bright Amish girls, available at
far less cost, could have functioned at a higher level. Financial
considerations may have played some part in the decision to
hire no more state-approved teachers, for the school committee
was having to pay considerably higher salaries as time went on.
Disillusionment was almost certainly involved. Apparently the
Amish were complying with a law that did not make sense
to them partly in deference to public officials they trusted and
admired. They had particular respect for Kaskadden. But now they
felt they had been betrayed. Perhaps the convictions of the Amish
School Committee members concerning the religious defensibility
of certified teachers did genuinely change when a traumatic
series of events forced a reexamination of relationships between
God and Caesar. Some local citizens insist that Dan Borntreger
lost face in his community when his compact with public officers
turned out to be worthless, and he had to take some kind of
dramatic counteraction to reestablish his influence. Or a complex
combination of factors may have been involved.

Whatever their logic, the Amish played into the hands of
their antagonists by suddenly refusing to comply with the law
requiring certified instructors. Previously, hostile Hazletonians
lacked a legal reason for demanding action against the Plain People.
The Amish had bypassed several requirements of the school code,
but common citizens had no right to inspect private schools;
so most shortcomings were largely unnoticed. Whenever violations
were visible, as when buildings went unpainted or vacations began
too early, neighbors would complain, public educators would issue
a few threats, and the faults would be rectified. For a brief
period during September 1961, one school was staffed by an

uncertified teacher, but the Buttons noticed right away (a buggy
rather than an automobile was parked outside), the county
superintendent uttered thunder, and the situation was soon
corrected. But in permanently renouncing state-approved instructors
in the fall of 1962, the Amish gave their angry neighbors the
clear-cut instance of law-breaking they had sought. There was an
immediate, vehement demand that the Amish be prosecuted.

FROM BAD TO WORSE

As pressure mounted for action against the Amish, local
leaders at first avoided involvement by raising jurisdictional
questions. In time, the officials were forced into several futile
legal proceedings, interspersed with scapegoating and efforts to
achieve a compromise. But the problem only worsened.

The reorganized Oelwein Community School District,
which has responsibility for enforcing the compulsory attendance
law, includes parts of Fayette and Buchanan counties. Since
the district headquarters are in Fayette County, the attorney
for that county acts for the school board on most litigative
issues. But Hazleton's two Amish schools are in Buchanan County.
Each county attorney argued, then, that the other was responsible
to move against the defiant parents. Finally, someone thought of
requesting a ruling from Des Moines, whereupon the Buchanan
County Attorney, then William O'Connell, was identified as the
proper person to act as prosecutor. O'Connell insisted, however,
that he could do nothing until some school officer filed
informations against the Plain People. Under fire from citizens
who wanted immediate action, he protested that Oelwein school
board members, who didn't "have guts enough" to do their duty,
were to blame for the delay. Oelwein officials announced that
the county school superintendent should be the one to institute
proceedings. While the law merely *permitted* local school boards
to prosecute in such cases, they argued speciously, it *required*
the county superintendent to do so. Oelwein leaders also insisted
that they could do nothing until state agencies took the first step.
The attorney general and state superintendent of schools,

in turn, declared that the controversy was purely local in character and as such was a matter for local people to handle.

On the morning of September 25, 1962, Kaskadden complained to Bruce Girton, then school board president, of exhaustion and dizziness. Reorganization had burdened Kas heavily, along with lengthy and frequent board meetings to deal with the Amish problem. On the evening of that day, he puttered a little in his basement, came upstairs, and slumped dead into a chair. At an emergency board meeting the next morning, Arthur Sensor was appointed acting superintendent.

After Kaskadden's death, the Amish were less hopeful of reaching an equitable settlement with the authorities, for Kas was one of the few school officers they trusted. Even today, they attempt to rationalize the broken agreement in terms of Kaskadden's passing, preferring to ignore the fact that the board had changed its tune when Kas was at the helm. Intransigence set in on both sides. The Oelwein board began to deny there ever was a behind-the-scenes arrangement with the Plain People. On November 29, 1962, the *Daily Register* reported, "At least one news agency stated to Sensor that they had conclusive evidence that the Oelwein Community School District had promised the Amish two schools in the Amish settlement. The school board felt that this and other similar statements were untrue." In the next issue of the same newspaper, Board President Bruce Girton "emphatically denied that any deal had been made with the Amish and said there had absolutely been no doublecross in the situation." Several local people think it conclusive to point out that no one had authority, before the reorganized Oelwein district was formed, to make a legally binding covenant in behalf of the district. Neither Kaskadden, his board members, nor the Amish ever pretended the compact was legally binding. It was an informal understanding that public officials as individuals promised to honor. The Plain People, accustomed to loaning money to each other over a handclasp, simply relied on the personal integrity of these officials. According to some observers, the Oelwein board's reluctance to prosecute the Amish was partly attributable to embarrassment, for the Amish kept mentioning the shattered covenant.

J. J. Jorgensen, then Buchanan County Superintendent of
Schools, was the first educator to yield to demands for punitive
action, possibly because his board, unlike Arthur Sensor's,
was drawn entirely from the county where the hostility was
centered. Jorgensen did not proceed on his own volition.
According to several observers, he was a tired, noncommittal
office holder who hoped nothing controversial would arise to
disturb his plans for retirement. On November 24, 1962,
acting on information filed by Jorgensen, Buchanan County
Attorney William O'Connell prosecuted ten Amishmen before a
justice of the peace for failing to send their children to schools
with certified teachers. All ten were fined. Eight refused to pay
on religious grounds and served three days behind bars. Newspapers
across the continent published pictures of black-bonnetted Amish
mothers on the way to visit their husbands in jail. Local officials
were deluged with insulting letters. Soon there was talk of how
O'Connell was "bungling the Amish affair." Next, O'Connell
sought an injunction to close the Old Order schools, but the
district court pointed out, somewhat tartly, that there was no
statutory basis for such action. In the next Republican primary,
O'Connell's handling of the case was widely debated, and he was
trounced. Other men, sobered by these events, sought the more to
avoid involvement. To act against the Plain People was
"quicksand," "political suicide," "taking a bear by the tail."
The controversy was "one of those affairs that tar everyone with
the same brush."

In January 1963, at the urging of the beleaguered county
superintendent, the Oelwein board offered once more to run the
two Amish schools temporarily if Dan Borntreger's group would
agree to send all seventh- and eighth-grade students to Hazleton
at once and all other pupils within two years. The proposal,
no different from previous ones, was rejected. In October 1963,
the attorney for the Amish, William Sindlinger, sought
unsuccessfully in district court to have his clients exempted from
the law demanding certified teachers. Arguing that "this may be
a way out of the impasse for us all," he tried to persuade the
Oelwein board not to oppose the petition. The board refused.
Its position was becoming more rigid.

In September 1964, another compromise was attempted. At the suggestion of State Superintendent Paul Johnston, the Oelwein board offered to provide special ungraded classrooms for Amish children in the Hazleton school on a one-year trial basis. The Amish would not concur. Later, officials proposed that Borntreger's people hire a certified Amish teacher (a virtually unheard-of species) from Kalona, Iowa. The Amish School Committee interviewed the teacher and announced that he was "not our kind of Amishman." If forced to accept a certified instructor, Borntreger said, his group would prefer a total outsider.

The turning point in the long series of delaying actions came in September 1965. An Oelwein school board member whose term was not expiring resigned, and several others decided not to seek reelection; so four new members were placed on the seven-man body. The Amish affair had been an important behind-the-scenes issue in the election. In response to adverse national publicity, sentiments in Oelwein had become less sympathetic toward the Amish. The new members of the board had implied they would deal more firmly than their predecessors with the Plain People. At the first meeting of the reconstituted board, the new Buchanan County attorney, Harlan Lemon, was present. Repeatedly during his campaign he had promised "to enforce all laws," and he urged the Oelwein board to file informations against the Amish immediately. Almost simultaneously, a leader of the antireorganization faction in Hazleton announced that he would ask a court to remove Sensor from office for failing to make the Amish obey the school code. In the words of Sensor, "We didn't give him a chance to act. We acted first." Oelwein officials filed informations against the offending Old Order parents in the court of Justice of the Peace Minnie Wengert.

For a number of weeks, local leaders had known they were in for trouble. In response to their call for aid, Iowa's attorney general, then Lawrence Scalise, had summoned County Attorney Harlan Lemon and two Amish representatives to Des Moines "to work something out." Scalise first persuaded the Amish to accept certified teachers once more—so long as the Amish School Committee did not have to pay the salaries. (The Amish often make a distinction between what they may do for themselves and what it is permissible, under duress, to let Caesar do.) Then Superintendent Sensor of Oelwein was convinced, according to Scalise, that the only way out of the impasse was for the Oelwein board to take over the Amish schools quietly and run them for two years, during which time a more permanent solution could be found. For example, two Amish teachers might take some courses by correspondence, qualifying for special certificates that would be valid only in Old Order schools. Scalise emphasized, however, that hotheads in Hazleton and Oelwein would quickly sabotage the arrangement if it were publicized before the board had acted conclusively. Scalise insists that Sensor agreed to bring the matter before his board with as little fanfare as possible.

As it turned out, the board meeting at which Scalise's proposal was considered was a virtual press conference. While the board was still in session, Scalise phoned County Attorney Lemon to see what progress was being made. Lemon observed that reporters had been invited to the discussion and that the board was about to reject the proposal. Scalise relayed a plea to the board that they defer action until he had a chance to discuss the matter with them personally. Then he talked to the members of the press by telephone, begging them not to publicize the matter until it had been resolved. When he watched the news on television that night, the issue was exposed in great detail.

Still not willing to concede defeat, Scalise pressed for a closed consultation with the Oelwein board. The meeting was scheduled for September 28. In the meantime, the Oelwein board decided the meeting should be held in public "so everything will be in the open." Plans for the discussion with Scalise were revealed in a major story in the Oelwein *Daily Register*. But Scalise was not informed of the change. A Democrat, he was widely disliked in Oelwein, a Republican stronghold, not only because of his political affiliation but also because he had publicly castigated Oelwein officials for their "inflexible approach" to the Amish problem. On September 28, Scalise flew to Oelwein, hurried to Sensor's long office, where the board usually met, and chatted with Sensor while munching a sandwich (he had missed dinner). When time for the meeting approached, Sensor

announced that it was open to the public and ushered Scalise onto
the platform of the junior high school auditorium nearby. A
belligerent crowd of three hundred had gathered. What happened
next has been generally described as a "three-ring circus."
Board members and people in the audience fired a barrage of
loaded questions at Scalise, and each time he winced or faltered,
the crowd clapped and cheered. Scalise said later he had "lost
fifteen pints of blood" at the meeting, and felt Sensor was
responsible. Sensor insists, however, that he tried to persuade the
board to hold a closed meeting. A "side show" of this kind is
always a mistake, he says. He would never deliberately subject
anyone to the embarrassment Scalise suffered that evening.

    After an hour or so of high humor at Scalise's expense,
the board summarily rejected his proposal. Board members claim
that he was simply trying to trick them into taking over the two
Amish schools, establishing a practice that would be difficult to
abandon. Near the end of the meeting, Scalise said he had been
asked for advice in a strictly local affair, had offered assistance
in good faith, and had received only insults as a result. From now
on, he declared, Oelwin could worry about its own problem.
He would have nothing more to do with it. "But don't come
running to me for help the next time you get yourselves in a jam!"

    Shortly thereafter, Justice of the Peace Minnie Wengert began
to process charges against the Amish in her renovated porch in
Hazleton. For more than three weeks, fourteen bearded Amishmen
showed up each night, Monday through Friday, beaming good will
and bearing gifts of garden produce for Mrs. Wengert, the sheriff,
and other officials. As if to provide a little variety, Adin Yuzy
stayed home from time to time and had to be fetched by the
sheriff. It soon became the custom to arrive early and stay late,
for Mrs. Wengert would pour coffee and the antagonists would
munch and visit. But occasionally a certain bitterness was
detectable beneath the outward amity, and a few of the smiles
came out a bit grotesque. At 7:30 each evening, officials testified
that the Amish had once more refused to obey the law, the Amish
acknowledged that the charge was true, each defendant was
fined $20 plus $4 costs, and each refused to pay on religious
grounds. Occasionally Dan Borntreger showed up (he was not a

defendant) to administer a lecture from Scripture, and Mrs.
Wengert retorted with some well-chosen Bible quotations of her
own. It was announced that the fines and costs would be
exacted at the end of each school day, indefinitely, until the
Plain People complied with the Iowa code. Furthermore, Amish
properties would soon be seized and sold to pay the levies.

A clever young man with a lean and hungry look, County
Attorney Harlan Lemon was in no mood to be accused, like his
predecessor, of botching the Amish issue. He sought, not
punishment, but compliance. As the weeks wore on, he worried.
The nightly sessions were robbing important leaders of an
unconscionable amount of energy and time, and the Amish
showed no sign of relenting. It would not take long at this rate
to ruin the Amish community financially, and the political
consequences of that eventuality were unthinkable. Lemon began
to explore ways of ending the impasse in off-the-record discussions
with Superintendent Sensor and two or three Amishmen who
secretly disagreed with the Amish School Committee and Dan
Borntreger. Toward the end of October, the Oelwein board
renewed its offer of an ungraded classroom for the Amish in
the Hazleton school on a one-year trial basis. The Plain People
again rejected the compromise, even when it was suggested that
their fines could be waived as a part of the package. Finally,
the behind-the-scenes negotiators agreed, according to Lemon and
Sensor, that everyone would save face if the Old Order pupils
were escorted to Hazleton in accordance with Iowa's truancy
statute. Since the Amish will not resort to violent resistance,
Borntreger would be powerless to prevent officials from
transporting the children to the public school and thus could
claim that he was overcome by force rather than modifying his
convictions. Those who disagreed with Borntreger would have
their way without causing a serious schism in their community.
Public officials would succeed in enforcing the law without
jailing or bankrupting the Plain People.

A plan was mapped out. Working sub rosa, the two or three
Plain People would prepare their brethren for the coming events.
Early one morning, public school busses would quietly arrive at
the Old Order schools. Amish leaders would remonstrate

appropriately, for the record. The children would be loaded onto buses in spite of the protests and taken to the public school. After a few days of ritual, a pattern of compliance would be set, and the trouble would all be over.

In the meantime, County Attorney Lemon phoned Attorney General Scalise about another matter, and in the process casually mentioned the strategy for dealing with the Amish. "What you do is strictly your own business," Scalise responded. "Count me out. Enforce the truance statute if that's what you want to do. But if you manhandle those little kids, you will be in trouble with the state!"

On Thursday evening, November 18, 1965, Lemon announced in Minnie Wengert's court that a school bus would call at the Amish homes and schools the next morning and take all the pupils to Hazleton, in keeping with the law. He requested that the Amishmen explain the situation to the children to avoid undue excitement. The fathers who were present neither assented nor protested. The Amish often refuse to respond to a new proposal until they have a chance to confer with their leaders. But as the explosive showdown of the next two schooldays demonstrated, the two or three Plain People who previously agreed to this approach had certainly not spoken for their community!

THE TRUCE AND SETTLEMENT

When County Attorney Lemon, Superintendent Sensor, and Sheriff Beier arrived in Des Moines a few hours after the showdown at the Amish schoolhouse, Governor Hughes was out of town, not expected to return until late afternoon. Attorney General Scalise was still very angry with Sensor at the time, believing Sensor had doublecrossed him on at least two occasions. Scalise invited Lemon, a fellow Democrat, into his office, leaving Sensor and Beier to stew in the waiting room for nearly two hours. According to Scalise, Lemon said the group had come to ask that Scalise deputize one officer for each Amish child involved in the controversy or that the governor call out an equal number of national guardsmen. With one official to escort each Old Order pupil to the Hazleton public school, the trouble could quickly

be ended. Scalise responded that the idea was unspeakably stupid
and threatened again to take strong action if any Amish
youngsters were handled roughly. William Sindlinger, the attorney
for the Plain People, reports that the three officials were overheard
discussing this plan before they left the North School to journey
to the capital. Sensor and Beier deny that such a proposal was
ever considered, and Lemon has recently been unavailable for
comment.

At any rate, Scalise made sure that Sensor and Beier were
kept waiting long enough to feel insulted. When he had nothing
more to discuss with Lemon, Scalise busied himself with other
matters. Finally, his secretary reported that Sensor was threatening
to leave for Oelwein. Scalise summoned all the newsmen he
could find, ushered them into his office along with Sensor and
Beier, and proceeded to discuss emphatically and at great length
the unreasonable approach he thought Sensor and other local
officials had been adopting.

Around 4:00 P.M., Governor Hughes returned to his office.
He closeted himself with Lemon and Scalise, leaving Sensor and
Beier waiting once more. A little later, he proposed to Sensor
and Beier, first privately and then at a press conference, that a
moratorium of at least three weeks be called to permit him to
explore alternatives. Sensor and Beier had little choice but to
agree, and the Oelwein board later ratified the arrangement
reluctantly. During the moratorium there were to be no further
attempts to take the Amish children to Hazleton, and the
prosecution of their parents was to cease.

Shortly thereafter, Buchanan County officials announced that
grain and livestock belonging to nine Amish farmers would be
auctioned to pay the fines and court costs that were levied before
the moratorium began. Amid an outcry that the Amish had again
been betrayed, the governor observed that, though the action
of the county leaders was unfortunate and would "not create
any good will," technically the truce had not been violated.
At the last moment, an anonymous donor in Des Moines came
forward with $1,511 so the sale could be cancelled (some people
believe the governor raised this money). In January 1966,
two businessmen from Independence, Iowa, eleven miles south

of Hazleton, donated $282 to prevent another auction. A few days later, 980 bushels of Amish corn were sold to pay fines and court costs, and further auctions were threatened. But before long the governor remitted more than $8,000 that the Amish still owed the state. Some local leaders are unhappy about this. "The governor made asses of us. We went to court every night for all those weeks, and nothing ever came of it."

On January 10, 1966, Governor Hughes conferred separately with Amish leaders and the Oelwein school board. Three state patrol cars and two dozen newsmen were at the Oelwein airport when his Piper Aztec touched down, and a long procession trailed behind as he sped down the dusty roads to Dan Borntreger's house. Several Amishmen drove up in buggies to attend the meeting, some came on foot, and a few were dropped off from automobiles driven by their neighbors. The conference lasted for nearly two hours, while the blankets on the horses flapped in the breeze, the windmill creaked, and sheep and pigs meandered in the fields. Finally the governor emerged and drove to Amish School No. 1, half a mile west. There he was photographed talking to Andy Kaufman while the American flag flew upside down nearby. No insult or distress signal was intended. The Amish are not too attentive to such details.

In the afternoon, Governor Hughes spoke briefly to students in Oelwein's junior high school auditorium, remarking that "we must respect the right of others to live differently, . . . if it is an honest and decent way of life." Then he met for two hours with the Oelwein board around the long table in Arthur Sensor's office. Simultaneously, Adin Yutzy, whom the sheriff had fetched to court on several occasions, was auctioning his last pieces of farm equipment before moving to Wisconsin. He wanted to get away from all the trouble.

As it turned out later, the Amish agreed that day to lease their schools to the public school district for a nominal sum; the public school board promised to supply certified teachers to the two schools for the rest of 1965-66 and during 1966-67; and since the board refused to pay the salaries of the two teachers, the governor promised to find funds for this purpose elsewhere. In a signed statement, the school board went on record that "adjustments will be made in the curriculum offered and in the teaching aids and methods used in these two schools, consistent with Iowa law, to avoid conflict with Amish religious beliefs." The Amish promised that, since the schools would be publicly maintained during this period, no religion would be taught.

In search of the needed money, Governor Hughes asked Francis Keppel, then U.S. Commissioner of Education, if federal funds could be made available. Keppel pointed out that the church-state overtones of the Amish problem made it too sensitive for Washington to handle and suggested that the Danforth Foundation of St. Louis might help. By February 22, 1966, Danforth consented to provide the needed $15,000, and the agreement was publicized. The governor said he would ask the 1967 session of the Iowa Legislature to create a fund for school boards that wished to make special schools available to minorities like the Amish.

During the rest of the 1965-66 school year, certified teachers were in charge of instruction in the two schools, with the former Amish teachers as assistants. The arrangement led to difficulty, for the Old Order assistants sometimes contradicted statements by the teachers in charge. During 1966-67, the Amish permitted the certified teachers to proceed alone, and few problems arose. The Plain People objected to some extent when they saw that a course in social studies was to be offered, emphasizing that they would prefer history and geography to be taught separately. The *Fayette County Union* commented: "Most of us had the impression old Dan [Borntreger] came away from the bargaining table with everything but Governor Hughes' suspenders. Now it would appear he wanted them too." To avoid trouble, the public school authorities refrained from introducing science into the curriculum of the two schools.

In its 1967 session, the Iowa legislature refused to establish the special fund requested by Governor Hughes, apparently in response to the wishes of the state superintendent, associations of educators, and other conservative elements. For a time, in fact, the lawmakers were unwilling to make any concessions to the Amish. The governor was forced to circumvent these tendencies. He established a special advisory committee of influential citizens who, armed with new arguments and evidence from interested scholars, worked through key senators and representatives to arrange an amendment to the state's minimum educational standards law. It was provided that religious groups could apply for exemption from the provisions of this law. Exemption would be granted for two-year periods only, and only at the discretion of the state superintendent, who had shown little aversion to the treatment the Amish had been accorded thus far. But so long as national outrage seems certain to be aroused by further heavy-handedness with the Plain People, peace may be maintained. At this writing, Hazleton's two Amish schools have been granted the necessary exemption and have reopened under the tutelage of uncertified instructors from the Amish community.

AN ANALYSIS

The action against the Amish in Hazleton was prompted, it seems clear, not by concern for the well-being of Amish children, but by antagonism. The Iowa school code, however it was intended, provided a convenient instrument for the persecution of an unpopular minority, harnessing public power to the wagon of local prejudice. But could public officials have condemned the Amish schools on more rational grounds? How should educators view the way the Plain People prepare their young for adulthood?

On the surface, the issue seems clear-cut. Demanding that all children be given a "decent education," numerous state legislatures have established minimum standards for all schools. Repeatedly the Old Order Amish violate these standards. A small but growing proportion of Amish children are in public schools; however, the private elementary schools most Amish youngsters attend are of the primitive one-room variety described earlier. To stay out of the forbidden secondary grades, many Amish boys and girls begin school a year later than usual, repeat the eighth grade, attend part-time Amish "vocational high schools" —which some states refuse to recognize—or simply drop out, compulsory attendance laws notwithstanding.

With their education thus limited, the Amish cannot produce

their own certified teachers; so when they refuse to hire personnel
from the outside there is trouble, at least in states like Iowa
that require certified instructors for all schools. But often many
other state standards are violated. During 1959-60, after visiting
twenty-two Amish elementary schools, representatives of Ohio's
Department of Education judged all to be in violation of
eighteen of the state's thirty-nine minimum standards for nonpublic
schools, while only one standard (relating to length of school day)
was met by all twenty-two. All of the schools were reported
as failing, for example, to comply with state demands for a term
of specified length; teacher personnel records; graded courses of
study in language arts, geography, history, mathematics, natural
science, health and physical education, fine arts, first aid, safety,
and fire prevention; provisions for staff growth; teaching aids,
adequate instructional materials; supplementary textbooks and
references; and satisfactory heat, light, ventilation, water, and
sanitary facilities. When nine Amish "vocational high schools"
were visited, all nine were judged to violate seventy-nine
secondary school standards. According to Ohio authorities,
the Amish schools have not improved significantly since then.

But contrary to a common view, this noncompliance
represents more than stubbornness or stupidity. It is calculated to
preserve the highest Amish values. At the heart of the Amish
culture, reinforced by religious tenets and a long history of
persecution, is the view that the larger society is evil. The Amish
are taught to keep themselves peculiar—a separated people.
They are knit together by kinship, common unquestioned values,
and customs that mark them off visibly from everyone else.
By emphasizing mixed farming as a way of life, they limit the
need for outside contacts. Reliance on horse-and-buggy
transportation keeps the basic social unit small, facilitating
surveillance of behavior. Community norms prescribe ways of
acting in such detail that most early symptoms of rebellion are
detected. The *streng meidung*—the strict shunning of those who
violate Amish rules, even by spouses and other members of the
immediate family—is a powerful enforcer of obedience.

Like other social systems, Amish society is organismic,
composed of mutually dependent parts. Alter one component

and the rest will change in response, often in irreversible, self-reinforcing fashion. Allow automobiles, radios, telephones, and modernized clothing, and the individual feels less distinct from the dominant social order and starts to assimilate its values. Take away farming as the predominant occupation, and exposure to alien folkways is vastly increased, for more complex callings demand more formal education and bring interdependence in their wake. Inure the child to the consolidated public school, replete with such luxuries as bus rides, plumbing, and electrical devices, and he is less likely to tolerate the taboos of his culture as an adult; furthermore, his peers and teachers will often influence him to defect. Give him a modern secondary education, or even too elaborate an elementary education, and he will frequently gain aspirations for, and access to, pursuits that are outlawed for an Amishman. Expose him too long to the lure of learning and he will hunger for the higher education that will alienate him still further from his origins.

On the other hand, rapid assimilation is not the only danger confronting the Old Order. If the Amish permit no adaptation to their changing environment, their culture will soon prove unworkable and the community will disintegrate. This eventuality may be most imminent when the Amish are threatened, for then, rather typically, they seem to emphasize norms that otherwise would have been abandoned; as a result, disruptive pressures are created, particularly for the young. When overt attacks cease, the settlements appear to strike a more realistic balance between rigidity and capitulation. It is in these relatively peaceful situations, one suspects, that the Amish are most likely to perpetuate important cultural distinctions while avoiding alienation, marginality, and anomie.

One fact is often ignored by public officers: In terms of the Amish culture, the Plain Peoples' approach to education may be one of the most effective yet devised. Their success in training the young to be farmers has impressed many agricultural experts. Unemployment, indigence, juvenile delinquency, and crime are surprisingly infrequent. Amish prosperity and self-sufficiency are legendary. These are not the characteristics of a preparation for adulthood that has failed.

Like Iowa, nevertheless, most states with Old Order Amish populations have attempted, at one time or another, to compel the Amish to meet the educational demands that apply to everyone else. But the statutes in these states rarely empower public authorities to close substandard schools; the only means of enforcement is to prosecute, under compulsory attendance laws, parents who send their children to these schools. When Amish parents are fined, jailed, or deprived of their property, those who have acted against them are blistered by angry protests from people sympathetic to the Amish, as in Iowa, and nasty publicity results. Elected officials soon find it morally or politically prudent to arrange a truce.

The Ohio situation illustrates the impasse that usually results from attempts to impose customary educational standards on the Amish. Officials of Ohio's Department of Education insist that virtually all Amish schools in the state are operating in defiance of the statutes, but these officials are painfully aware of popular support for the Amish and despair of enforcing the law without authority to close the schools rather than prosecuting the parents.

Until exemptions were provided for Amish schools in Iowa, Pennsylvania's attitude was clearly the most liberal of all. Long ago, after several embarrassing confrontations had occurred, George Leader, then governor, arranged a reinterpretation of the school code to legitimize the Amish educational pattern. Since that time, Amish elementary schools have been required to maintain school days and terms of standard length and to file adequate attendance reports, but practically no other stipulations are made—teachers, for instance, need not be state-certified. Children who complete the eighth grade and are at least fourteen years old may enter the Amish "school-work program" in "vocational high schools" until they reach the legal school-leaving age of sixteen. In this program, students perform farm and household duties under parental guidance and attend classes for a few hours each week. Many educators feel, however, that Pennsylvania has thus abdicated its responsibility to see that all future citizens receive an adequate education.

In a few areas, as in school districts immediately west of

Hazleton, Iowa, a third policy has been adopted with some success. The Amish are provided with small public schools in their rural settlements rather than being assigned to consolidated schools in neighboring towns. (In a few instances the Hutterite colonies in Montana enjoy the same privilege.) The boards of these public schools seek teachers sympathetic to the Amish position and in numerous other ways ensure that the religious sensibilities of pupils and parents are not offended. The arrangement provides Amish youngsters with state-certified teachers and sometimes with more modern curricula and facilities than are found in private Amish schools.

Some legal scholars see such an explicit concession to a particular religious group as an establishment of religion, forbidden by the First Amendment. But the approach may be constitutional if viewed, not as a set of exceptions for a single sect, but as simply one application among many of a universally valid principle. To be effective, educational programs must be fitted to the cultures of the pupils served, whether these pupils come from Amish, Hutterite, Puerto Rican Catholic, upper-class WASP, or lower-class Negro backgrounds. However, some Amish groups balk at a compromise of this type. Not only does it expose the young to teachers with alien values, but, unlike schools in the days before school district reorganization, the schools in question are governed by boards rarely drawn from the immediate communities.

Public school officers, and even the courts, are often guilty of simplistic comparisons between public and Amish schools. In Ohio's Hershberger case, for instance, advantages unique to the public school were emphasized; advantages unique to Amish education were brushed aside. What happened within the four walls of the public schoolhouse was compared merely with what happened within the four walls of the Amish schoolhouse, and the fact that Amish children are educated largely outside school walls was deemed irrelevant. The Amish community assigns only limited functions to formal instruction, requiring the school merely to teach the three R's. Yet away from the schoolhouse, each child undertakes a series of tasks under parental tutelage.

Kitchens, stables, markets, and fields—not classrooms—are the principal educational facilities.

Many public educators would be elated if their programs were as successful in preparing students for productive community life as the Amish system seems to be. In fact, while some public schoolmen strive to outlaw the Amish approach, others are being forced to emulate many of its features. As tax-supported education struggles with the dropout and potential dropout, it is introducing sizable components outside school walls, as in the Job Corps and many other work-study programs. Investigations of teaching and learning indicate that much more differentiation of instruction is necessary, and schools are being criticized justly for their standardization and lack of adaptability.

Furthermore, serious attitudinal and cognitive consequences might ensue if Amish children were suddenly bussed into unaccustomed surroundings to be taught by teachers unsympathetic toward Amish customs, to associate with peers who maintain an incompatible life outlook, and to study subjects in which they have little or no interest. The practice implies the same blind application of inappropriate treatments to which the culturally deprived in the great cities have been subjected for so many years. There is no basis in educational theory, research, or experience for insisting, as critics of Amish education frequently do, that the within-four-walls approach of the typical public school is the only way adequately to educate the nation's future citizens. At times a nonpublic school that provides a particular group of students with a thoroughly appropriate preparation for the adult life they will lead may differ so fundamentally from nearby public schools that the notion of parity is farcical. When are oranges and orangutangs equivalent?

But even if the prevailing approach to regulation of nonpublic schools is ill-conceived, some kind of control may be needed. The most common rationale for this control inheres in the view that the state must, as a means of self-protection, require for all children an education essential to good citizenship. The state courts have defended this concept in many compulsory-attendance cases, holding that an education is not so much a right guaranteed the individual as a duty imposed on him for the public good.

Assuming the state must protect itself, one consideration is basic: Does the Amish educational approach represent anything more than the reasonable discretion of parents? Does it preclude anything plainly essential to good citizenship or include anything manifestly inimical to the general welfare? Since the recipients of Amish schooling function so well in the Amish communities and the larger society suffers no significant threat in the process, the answer has to be *no*. Unlike other rural youth, the Amish do not gravitate in large numbers to the cities, where their lack of a highly developed formal education might create serious problems. Individuals almost never leave the Old Order Amish culture for the nation's mainstream. The normal movement, accomplished over several generations, is from Old Order Amish to "Church Amish" to Amish Mennonite and then through a sequence of increasingly modern Mennonite persuasions. As some Mennonites put it, "We are all on the same train, but the Old Order Amish are in the last car." The existing evidence shows no trace of former Amishmen who are struggling unsuccessfully to adjust in the outside world, perhaps partly because they take so long to reach the head of the train and partly because of the habits of self-reliance, hard work, and frugality that are so central in the Amish and Mennonite cultures.

In most respects the Amish must be viewed as good citizens. Their aversion to political activity, social security, and military service is probably more than balanced by the thought-provoking dissent they contribute to our national dialogue. On the whole, it would be difficult to identify any other ethnic group that has done so little to burden society. If the Amish schools may be outlawed, why not the Amish communities? If it is permissible to live as an Amishman in the United States, why is it not equally permissible to prepare to live as an Amishman?

As a second basis for state intervention, it is maintained that every child should have access to the occupational and ideological options that a modern education make available, regardless of parental preferences. One is inclined to be cynical, however, when many state authorities express this concern. There is something fishy about a legislator or schoolman who weeps over the limited opportunities of Amish youth and yet shows no pangs of conscience concerning the gross inequities that discriminate against the poor in public education. The state courts, moreover, have been too preoccupied with the self-protection prerogatives of the states to champion individual rights in education.

Nevertheless, the issue of freedom of choice must be taken seriously. With a typical Amish education, the individual would have difficulty moving into the more complex vocations. To expose the youngster to one life view exclusively during the formative years is virtually to coerce him into adopting that view. But while the public school may broaden horizons in the world of work, it is hardly a neutral forum for competing concepts in religion, politics, economics, and other controversial spheres. As a thousand battles in the courts and elsewhere have shown, attempts to make public education neutral in religion and in other ideological particulars have raised problems of the profoundest sort, and the eventual outcome of the efforts is very much in doubt.

Public schools—like Amish, Hutterite, Black Muslim, Lutheran, Catholic, Jewish, Greek Orthodox, and Seventh Day Adventist schools—seem inevitably the servants of their constituencies, reflecting the dominant values of the subcultures they serve. (Ask any pacifist who has attended a public school in wartime.) What agency of the state, then, may be trusted to select an educational format so superior or allegedly neutral that it may be imposed on every child? The destinies of the young will often be misguided by parents, but this state seems far less lethal than the alternative of giving government the ultimate power of indoctrination.

Furthermore, if the state legislatures are genuinely concerned about maximizing the choices available to Amish youth, appropriate steps can be taken that do not infringe the basic rights of parents and threaten to create a new collection of maladjusted, miseducated youngsters. To mention just one possibility: The state could provide special supplementary educational opportunities for defecting Amishmen who wish to acquire the skills and understandings they will need in the larger world. Such programs should represent no inordinate burden.

Financially, the costs should be far less than those that would be incurred in educating all Amish children in public schools. Changes in occupation and way of life will be increasingly common in the future, and large numbers of citizens—not just a few erstwhile Amishmen—will require periodic retraining.

It is sometimes argued, finally, not that Amish education is a serious menace to the state or the child, but that the nation would be better off if all cultural backwaters, religious enclaves, and social classes were eliminated. Whites, according to this standpoint, must not be permitted to live entirely apart from Negroes. The wealthy must not be allowed to maintain a lofty isolation from the poor. Religious minorities must be brought into the mainstream of modern society. It is one thing, however, to forbid invidious distinctions in public functions and quite another to stifle self-determination in private affairs, when the individual infringes no rights of others.

To a large extent our form of government presupposes that rationality will win, in the long run, if the market of orthodox and unorthodox ideas is unrestricted. Over the centuries, important contributions have been made by groups that were at such marked variance with the established order as to need some degree of insulation to survive. In retrospect, the efforts of authorities to enforce, in private spheres, their concepts of the good tend to assume a bloody hue. In the words of the Supreme Court, "Those who begin coercive elimination of dissent soon find themselves exterminating dissenters. Compulsory unification of opinion achieves only the unanimity of the graveyard."

4

The Persecution of LeRoy Garber[1]
Donald A. Erickson

Kansas v. *Garber* might have been a landmark case in
the long history of Amish school litigation. Instead it
became simply another in a long series of legal defeats for
the Amish. Professor Erickson highlights the issues—and
misguided assumptions—which led to the final doleful
outcome.

This is a short, unfunny story about an Old Order Amishman,
his teen-age daughter, and a county superintendent of schools,
based on interviews with seventy-three people who were in a
position to shed light on the incident.[2]

I met the superintendent in Kansas a little more than a year
ago. He was elected to the job, he reported, largely because he
was popular among the farmers in the area, whose votes were
decisive, and because of his work for the party over the decades.
His salary was small for a professional educator, and he was
almost ready to retire. Recent years had been difficult, he noted,
for the legislature kept strengthening local school districts and
reducing the authority of the county office. Now a man in
his position had little left to do.

Some two years earlier, in the spring of 1965, the Kansas legislature had raised the school-leaving age from fourteen to sixteen. When school opened in the fall, the superintendent decided to see whether the Old Order Amish were obeying the new law. Finding three youngsters, not yet sixteen, who were not attending classes, he threatened to corral the parents of all three. When the parents did not capitulate, he decided, with the county attorney, to take a carefully selected test case to court. Both officials said they were not acting in response to local pressure, and other evidence supported that contention. They showed no firm conviction that what they were doing would benefit Amish children; in private, in fact, they both expressed some doubt in this regard. A few local people accused the superintendent of a personal vendetta against the Amish. What is more likely, I suspect, is that he acted under the anxiety of having little to do. Like dozens of other county superintendents in the United States, he could have circumvented or ignored a school law that seemed inappropriate or absurd.

Of the three children on the superintendent's list, one would have turned sixteen by the time court action was under way. Another, he said, was so retarded mentally as to be excusable from school on that basis, though educators who knew the child deny that this was so. The youngster selected as the best case material was a bright young woman, barely fifteen, whose name was Sharon. On October 5, 1965 her father, LeRoy Garber, was served a notice of truancy. To avoid arrest, it declared, he must send his daughter to high school at once.

Wondering whether Sharon had been deprived of an education, as the truancy notice implied, I called one December night at the Garber home. It had no radio, no television, only books, newspapers, magazines, and the arts and crafts the family pursued firsthand. As I discovered later, the Garbers were voracious readers, frequent patrons of the Hutchinson Public Library. Little Anne, just turned six years, clambered on her father, varoomed a toy tractor across a table, and answered questions with precocious fluency. She had taught herself to read.

Sharon explained that she completed the eighth grade in 1964. She was under no obligation to continue in school, for the

new law had not been passed. The school-leaving age was still
fourteen. She loved learning but felt it wrong, as most Amish do,
to attend the public high school. With her father's encouragement,
she registered for a high school course offered by mail by the
American School in Chicago, probably the most reputable of
the nation's correspondence institutions. While working part-time
in a greenhouse, she completed the four-year curriculum in thirty
months. According to information filed at the time of the
district court trial, discussed later, her percentage average at the
American School was 95.69.

When he received the notice of truancy, Garber rushed for
advice to E. Dexter Galloway, an attorney in the nearby city of
Hutchinson. Galloway suggested that Garber do everything
religiously permissible to show his good faith. "If the county
officials see you are sincerely attempting to comply with the law,
they will probably back down," Galloway predicted. Garber
discussed with Sharon some possible ways of avoiding trouble.
As before, she thought it wrong to attend the public high school—
that its influence on several friends was regrettable. But to pacify
the authorities, she enrolled almost immediately in a "vocational
high school" called Harmony, operated by an Old Order Amish
group a few miles distant, near the tiny village of Yoder.
Limited by his religion to buggy travel, Garber paid a neighbor
to drive Sharon to Harmony and back each week. At the same
time, she continued her correspondence work.

HARMONY

Harmony was a strange, unorthodox school, established by
the Yoder Amish in response to the new Kansas law. The teacher
had only an eighth-grade education. The classes met one morning
a week. The program consisted mainly of projects which the
students pursued at home.

The County Superintendent had been wondering for weeks
what to do about this off-beat school, so ludicrously
unconventional. Now he could take no further action against
Garber without deciding whether Harmony was acceptable. It was
a farce, he announced—a subterfuge—no school at all. Its teacher

was incompetent. Before reaching this conclusion, the superintendent did not discuss the facilities and activities with the school board, enter the building, administer an achievement test, examine a text or workbook, question a pupil or parent, or observe the teacher.

Harmony's format was devised years earlier in Pennsylvania, in discussions between state officials and the "Plain People" themselves. The weekly three hours of classes were supplemented by a minimum daily hour of academic assignments at home. The projects in agriculture and homemaking were prescribed because of the school's vocational purpose—to produce Amish farmers and housewives. Few Old Order children aspire to other occupations or to life outside the Amish community. The most appropriate laboratories, consequently, were not classrooms but kitchens, stables, markets, and fields. The best vocational instructors? The parents themselves. Who else could impart the attitudes and skills of Amish farmers and housewives?[3]

Harmony's academic teacher, Amos P. Borntrager, was chosen for his straight-A record in the elementary grades and because he continued to read widely. I found him an engaging human being with a wry sense of humor. There was a beautiful atmosphere of well-being in his classroom. Especially in arithmetic, which they valued for its usefulness on the farm, the parents claimed their offspring were learning more rapidly than before. Borntrager spent two days per week, he said, grading the assignments his nine students turned in on Friday mornings. He demanded not merely answers but complete notes concerning the methods used, and he studied in detail the steps each student followed. Many people commented on the toughness of his assignments. He labored endlessly with youngsters who had problems, the parents reported, much in contrast with fully certified teachers in the public elementary school these students attended earlier. . . .

In talking with personnel managers nearby, I discovered that the Plain People were in remarkable demand, their limited educations notwithstanding. Described by numerous employers as conscientious, energetic, and versatile, they were definitely preferred to run-of-the-mill high school graduates. (This situation would not be duplicated in distant cities, of course, where their reputation is unknown.)

As for Sharon Garber herself, she was employed part-time for two years at Ervin Stutzman's greenhouse. Sharon, said Stutzman, was "the best help we've had yet." She dreamed of a greenhouse of her own some day and devoured books on gardening in an effort to master the trade. He never had to explain anything twice to Sharon, said Stutzman. She typed his letters. When the adding machine was in use, she would figure sums mentally, using short-cut methods she had learned. She was the first employee he ever trusted with the critical task of planting. He would do so again if she were still available. Too bad she had to leave. Many informants described Sharon as a superb cook, skillful seamstress, unfailing green thumb. I could elicit no complaint from anyone who knew her concerning her character or competence. More recently, in an Amish periodical, she has published an account of her experiences in Kansas.[4] I wish the majority of high school graduates could write as well.

Sharon was not alone in pursuing correspondence courses. Many Plain People are now doing so, for in this way they can extend their knowledge while avoiding the social influences their elders fear. Upon reaching maturity, several have entered Kansas colleges on the basis of the General Educational Development (GED) high school equivalency examination. It was extremely unusual for an Amishman or Mennonite to fail this test, Kansas officials informed me, and those admitted to college on such a basis did at least as well as other groups. From four nearby Kansas colleges, I obtained the names and addresses of twenty-one Plain People who had been admitted on this basis during the previous ten years. Five addresses were incorrect. Of the twenty-one people I was able to contact, sixteen provided access to their academic records. Of the sixteen, four (25 percent) had earned an A average; thirteen (81 percent), at least a B average; and *all*, at least a C average. For not one of the sixteen was a grade below D recorded. One ranked first in a graduating class of fifty-six.[5]

The Amish vocational high school is itself a major adaptation, the first formalized instruction beyond the eighth grade the Old Order Amish have been willing to accept. Given encouragement rather than condemnation, they may strengthen this institution, perhaps gradually accentuating the academic studies as the need becomes more apparent.

But Reno County's officials would have no truck with that strange school the Yoder Amish started. It was not, the superintendent emphasized, "a regular parochial school." It did not matter, furthermore, that Sharon was halfway through her correspondence course, pursuing all the subjects the Kansas code required and more, achieving high grades, and reading extensively, as she had done for years. Her vocational adequacy meant nothing, nor her father's willingness to do whatever conscience would allow. So LeRoy Garber was arrested and taken to court.

"THE LAW IS A ASS, A IDIOT"

When the case came up, the county attorney could hardly argue that Sharon was denied an education; so he complained, like the superintendent, that she was educated in the wrong way. The district court agreed: "The defendant has not complied with Kansas compulsory school attendance laws. . . . To comply . . . such child must attend a private or parochial school having a school month consisting of four weeks of five days each of six hours per day during which pupils are under *direct* supervision of its teacher while they are engaged *together* in educational activities." When the Kansas Supreme Court reached an almost identical conclusion upon appeal, the Wichita *Eagle* paraphrased Charles Dickens's Mr. Bumble: "The law is a ass, a idiot."

At the same time, city schools all over the nation were trying "charm centers," volunteer tutoring, work-study arrangements, store-front schools, camping trips, "cultural enrichment" activities, schools with no classrooms at all, and dozens of other unconventionalities. A national task force on vocational technical education demanded "learning stations" out in the community. The North Central Accrediting Association revised its criteria to encourage instructional flexibility. Scholars urged that parents be given an important role in teaching their own children.

Most of these devices would be illegal under Kansas law as it
was interpreted in Garber's case.

One other point is pertinent: A great many studies—
among the Hutterites, the Menomini, the Hopi, the Sioux,
the Navaho, the Ojibwa, Pueblo groups, populations in the
American Arctic, Mennonite sects, and minorities in other parts
of the world—suggest that subcultures usually adjust best when
they do so voluntarily. Instead of blissful converts to middle-class
suburbia, forced assimilation most often produces "marginal men,"
tortured in a limbo between two societies but equipped to function
adequately in neither, tragically inclined to depression, suicide,
delinquency, crime, alcoholism, and unemployment. The results
are not the same for all minorities. When forced into the national
mainstream, some groups compete rather successfully for their
share of groceries and appliances. But the anguish of inner
conflict is practically universal. Who knows how much personal
and social harm would be caused by disruption of Amish
socialization patterns, to say nothing of the loss of cultural
diversity that would result? Who can assert that Sharon Garber
would have been better off, psychologically or academically,
if she had attended a regular high school in a nearby town?

The county superintendent declared, however, that these
questions were not his responsibility. He was merely enforcing
a law someone else had made. Whose responsibility were these
questions? In talking with state representatives, I discovered
that the legislature had passed the law without considering the
consequences for the Amish. It did not gather the relevant
evidence or debate the central dilemmas. The attitude of the
Kansas courts, incredibly, was that no constitutional issue of
religious liberty was involved. The legislature's discretion had been
reasonably exercised and hence should not be questioned. The
U.S. Supreme Court refused to hear the case, though not
necessarily approving the decisions made earlier.

Garber's lawyer, one surprisingly articulate school board
member, and LeRoy Garber himself were the only people I
encountered who seemed to have pondered to any extent the
critical questions in the case. That night in his home, Garber
was quick-witted, informed, and often eloquent, though obviously

distraught. Eyes flashing, beard stabbing the air, words tumbling
in a torrent, he reasoned concerning educational relevance,
religious liberty, cultural diversity. He cited Supreme Court
decisions on religion in public schools and the rights of defendants
in criminal proceedings. How, he demanded, could any judge
think his case less convincing than these? His daughter had been
educated. He had merely sheltered her, during adolescence,
from companions who might have an alienating influence.
In consequence, he had been hounded to court and fined. Was this
not a clear issue of religious liberty?

White prayer cap in place, Mrs. Garber pretended to be
busy with her mending. Her eyes flickered from husband to child,
her features reflecting each emotion our voices evoked. The place
was a mess, she said, with these stacks of boxes waiting for the
truck. They were moving away in search of peace. Their son,
Galen, was about to graduate from elementary school. Why should
they face the same difficulties with him that they had gone
through with Sharon? So they were harassed out of Kansas for
their religious convictions, and no one was required to defend
the ethics, constitutionality, or educational logic of the
harassment!

When I studied the Amish school controversy in Iowa in
1967, I learned of Adin Yutzy, whom the sheriff had fetched to
court on several occasions.[6] Yutzy paid a large fine, sold his farm,
and moved to New Glarus, Wisconsin, to get away from the
trouble. A few weeks ago the same Adin Yutzy announced that
he was leaving New Glarus, where the Amish are now being
prosecuted for their educational practices. There have been many
other migrations, at least partly in response to regulations that
conflict with Amish religion. In 1966 an entire community
left Arkansas for British Honduras. The Bearded Mennonites have
been scouting for land in Mexico, Paraguay, Venezuela, Costa Rica,
and Australia.

The decisions that uproot the LeRoy Garbers, the decisions
that threaten ethnic diversity, are they made through serious
debate in the public forum? Are they made by the nation's
wisest men, pondering deeply and long? Are they even made
through concern for the education of children? In the case of

LeRoy Garber, the answer was NO. In the Iowa controversy over
Amish education, which I examined in detail, the answer was an
emphatic NO. In encounters elsewhere which I have examined in
less depth and in instances which others have analyzed, the answer
seems to be NO. There is danger, then, that much beauty in
American life may be destroyed, not because thoughtful leaders
and informed citizens want this to be done, but through default.
In too many cases, the power to persecute is placed, through
ill-contrived laws, in the hands of minor officeholders—officials too
often motivated by local hostility, the desire to qualify public
schools for more state money, or in some situations, I fear,
the need to find something to occupy their time.

The tragedy of injustice, as Auden observed, is that it is
seldom noticed and rectified. "Even the dreadful martyrdom
must run its course anyhow in a corner, some untidy spot where
the dogs go on with their doggy life and the torturer's horse
scratches its innocent behind on a tree."[7]

5

A Chronology of Amish
Court Cases

Albert N. Keim

The Amish have been repeatedly prosecuted for their failure
to submit to compulsory attendance laws. What follows is not
a comprehensive list of all Amish court cases, but those listed
represent the more prominent cases and suggest the general response
of the courts to the Amish plight. The list fails to adequately
project the large number of local cases where Amishmen were
fined and jailed for refusal to send their children to school
beyond the eighth grade. The Amish response in the overwhelming
majority of cases was simply to pay the fine or serve the jail
sentence without a contest.

In 1966 the Amish gained an ally in their struggles with
school authorities from an unexpected quarter. The Reverend
William C. Lindholm, pastor of Holy Cross Evangelical Lutheran
Church near Livonia, Michigan, troubled by radio and newspaper
reports of the Amish school controversy in Iowa, decided to
take action on behalf of the Amish. In 1967 he established the
National Committee for Amish Religious Freedom. Distinguished
scholars, educators, churchmen, and lawyers joined the committee.

The committee's first intervention on behalf of the Amish
occurred in the *Kansas* v. *Garber* case in 1967. Subsequently it
was involved in other local school disputes, but its most significant
and successful effort came in the Wisconsin case. Under the

leadership of the Reverend Mr. Lindholm the committee engaged
the services of attorney William Ball of Harrisburg, Pennsylvania,
raised the money for the various appeals up through the Wisconsin
courts to the Wisconsin Supreme Court, and finally arranged
for the defense of the Amish before the U.S. Supreme Court.

To a large degree the work of the committee was carried
forward by the Revernd Mr. Lindholm. His persistence, in the face
of apathy and adversity, in raising funds, engaging attorneys,
and immersing himself in the Amish cause, was heroic.
The resolution of the Amish school problem in *Wisconsin* v. *Yoder*,
while the work of many people, is ultimately a vindication of
the faith and vision of this self-effacing, but resourceful, individual.

1927—Byler v. *State*, 26 Ohio App. 329, 157 N.E. 421 (1927).
Seth Byler was fined $25 by a justice of the peace
for failing to send his daughter to school beyond the eighth
grade as required by law. He appealed to the Common Pleas
Court which upheld the decision. The Court of Appeals
(Stark County, Ohio) reversed the decision on the basis of
a legal error by the Common Pleas Court.

*1937—*Federal District Court, Philadelphia, 1937.
Amish tried to halt construction of a consolidated
school They were upheld. The East Lampeter Township
School Board then appealed the decision to the Federal
Circuit Court of Appeals, which held in favor of the
school board.

*1937—*Chester County District Court, Pennsylvania, 1937.
Aaron King was brought to court for keeping his
fourteen-year-old daughter Rebecca at home from high
school. He was fined $2 and costs but refused to pay.
He was jailed for the night. He then appealed to the
Federal District Court in Philadelphia. King was convicted.

1948—Gingerich v. *State*, 226 Ind. 678, 83 N.E.2d 47 (1948).
Chester Gingerich refused to send his fourteen-year-old
son to high school thus violating the state school statute

requiring attendance between the ages of seven and sixteen.
The Jay Indiana Circuit Court fined Gingerich $200 and
sentenced him to sixty days at the Indiana State Farm,
the maximum punishment allowable under the statute.
Gingerich appealed to the Indiana Supreme Court, arguing
that the sentence was excessive and violated the state
constitution which prohibited excessive fines and cruel and
unusual punishments. The supreme court upheld the circuit
court decision.

1949—Commonwealth v. *Petersheim*, 70 Pa. O. and C. 432
(Somerset County Ct. 1949), appeal dismissed, 166 Pa. Super.
90, 70A.2d 395 (1950).

In this case the parents refused to send the children,
over fourteen, but under sixteen, to either public or parochial
school. A justice of the peace convicted the fathers of
violating the Pennsylvania compulsory attendance law.
On appeal the Amish asserted that Pennsylvania law did not
apply because the children were fifteen years old, were
engaged in farm or domestic work for their parents, and were
thus entitled to a permit exempting them from the
compulsory attendance law.

The court decided in favor of the Amish since to
enforce the law would be ". . . an abridgement and
infringement of their constitutional rights of liberty and
conscience" as based on the Fourteenth Amendment.

1950—Commonwealth v. *Beiler*, 168 Pa. Super. 462, 79 A.2d
134 (1951), affirming 52 Lanc. 167 (1950).

In this case the Pennsylvania Superior Court affirmed
the conviction of two Amish fathers whose children had not
continued school after the eighth grade. The court accepted
the genuineness of the Amish religious convictions regarding
education but went on to say: "Thus, we are squarely faced
with competing demands of the Commonwealth, evidenced
by its compulsory school law, and religious liberty, guaranteed
by the Constitution. Or to state the problem in other terms:
In the realm of secular education, which is paramount? The

State functioning according to democratic processes and
depending for its virility upon enlightened citizens; or
parents, whose deep and sincere religious convictions
reject advanced education as an encroachment upon their
way of life?"

The court then decreed that the state's interest was
paramount. The role of the state in enforcing compulsory
education must override parental claims based on religion
or conscience.

1955—Commonwealth v. *Smoker*, 54 Lancaster 188 (1954),
     aff'd 177 Pa. Super. 435, 110 A.2d 140 (1955).

Samuel Smoker was convicted for violating the
Pennsylvania school statute by keeping his fourteen-year-old
son, who had completed the eighth grade, out of school
without a permit. The Court of Quarter Sessions affirmed
the lower court decision.

1955—State v. *Hershberger*, 103 Ohio App. 188, 191, 144 N.E.
     2d 693, 697 (1955).

In 1954 John P. Hershberger and others, in Hardin
County, Ohio, established a private school in a one-room
frame building without light and heated by a coal stove.
The teacher, with no formal teacher training, had completed
the eighth grade. Hershberger was found guilty of failing
to cause his children to attend school as required by the
compulsory education laws of Ohio. The court insisted
religious freedom was not at issue. The defendant had a right
to establish a private school and send his children there.
The issue, said the court, was whether the instruction
provided in the private school was equivalent to the
instruction given in the public schools. The court felt that
the record showed that the instruction did not meet
state standards. Hershberger was convicted, fined $20,
and ordered to post a $100 bond with surety to ensure
compliance with the law.

1958—In re Sammy Hershberger, No. 2835, Wayne County,
Ohio Juvenile Court, January 29, 1958. *State* v. *Hershberger*,
77 Ohio L. Abs. 487, 150 N.E.2d 671 Wayne County
Juvenile Court 1958.

Hershberger and other Amishmen were charged with
child neglect for failing to send their children to school and
were ordered to surrender their children to the custody
of the Child Welfare Board. When the parents refused to
give up the children, they were cited for contempt and
sent to jail. Upon appeal Hershberger argued that his religious
convictions did not permit him to give up his child.
The court rejected the argument and upheld the contempt
order, finding no religious question involved. Later the
Wayne County Court of Appeal reversed the contempt
citations upon learning that the parents honestly did not
know where the children were.

1960—*State* v. *Glick et al.*, Medina County, Ohio, Court of
Common Pleas, Case No. 18191 (1960).

This case took place near Medina, Ohio, in 1960.
Local school authorities petitioned the Common Pleas
Court for an injunction to close a substandard Amish school
in the community. The case against the Amish was dismissed.

1962—*Jorgensen* v. *Borntrager*, No. 22904, Buchanan County, Iowa,
District Court (November 1962).

Local school authorities sought an injunction to close
the two local Amish parochial schools. The injunction was
denied on the grounds that the state did not have the power
to close private schools.

1966—*State* v. *Garber*, 197 Kan. 567, 419 P.2d 896 (1966).
certiori denied, 389 U.S. 51 (1967).

Amishman LeRoy Garber refused to send his fifteen-
year-old daughter to high school. The Kansas Supreme Court,
supporting a lower court decision, held that the state
compulsory education law was a valid exercise of the
police power, despite its acknowledged interference with the

practice of the Amish faith. The court adopted the
distinction between a right to believe and a right to act,
and concluded that the law was valid because it did not
infringe upon the right to worship or believe.

1971–State v. *Yoder*, 49 Wisconsin 2d 430, 182 N.W.2d
539 (1971).

In 1968 Jonas Yoder and two fellow Amishmen were
convicted in Green County court for violating the
Wisconsin compulsory school attendance statute. The circuit
court affirmed the lower court decree. The case was then
appealed to the Wisconsin Supreme Court which reversed
the conviction, arguing that the compulsory attendance law
imposed an excessive restriction on the free exercise of
religion of the Amish.

1972–Wisconsin v. *Yoder*, 406 U.S. 205 (1972).

The State of Wisconsin appealed the decision of the
Wisconsin Supreme Court to the U.S. Supreme Court.
On May 15, 1972, Chief Justice Warren Burger stated for
the Court: "A State's interest in universal education . . .
is not totally free from a balancing process when it
impinges on other fundamental rights and interests, such
as those specifically protected by the Free Exercise Clause
of the First Amendment and the traditional interest of
parents with respect to the religious upbringing of their
children." The Amish, the Court asserted, had convincingly
argued "that enforcement of the State's requirement of
compulsory formal education after the eighth grade would
gravely endanger if not destroy the free exercise of . . .
[Amish] religious beliefs." The Amish, the Court declared,
could not be forced to send their children to school beyond
the eighth grade.

6

The Cultural Context of the Wisconsin Case

John A. Hostetler

John A. Hostetler is a professor of sociology and anthropology at Temple University. He was born in an Amish home and understands the Amish as few people do. He has written numerous articles and books on the Amish, including *Amish Society* and *Children in Amish Society*.

In this essay he describes Amish cultural values and discusses several factors which made the Wisconsin case possible.

On hearing that the Supreme Court had upheld the Amish, defendant Jonas Yoder choked with deep emotion, then remarked, "I'm not one for making words, but it is a miracle from God. It's wonderful that a small people like us can still make a law in Washington. Now I just want to go back to farming."

A number of circumstances were favorable to the "miracle." There were previous legal attempts to protect the Amish. All had failed. Why did this far-reaching case emerge in a remote Amish community in Wisconsin and not in Lancaster County, Pennsylvania, or Holmes County, Ohio, where there are large concentrations of Amish? How was the Amish disdain for legal suits overcome?

An immediate factor in making the miracle possible was the National Committee for Amish Religious Freedom, organized by the Reverend William Lindholm in 1966, in the context of the school cases in Kansas (*Kansas* v. *Garber*) and in Iowa.[1] The committee placed the problem of Amish education on a broader base than was possible for the local Amish communities or the Mennonite brotherhood, thus giving it national perspective. Public opinion had become favorable to the Amish as a result of these previously widely publicized incidents.

The interest and ability of attorney William Ball of Harrisburg, Pennsylvania, contributed to the success of the case, particularly his understanding of historic religious freedom cases and his handling of the delicate aspects of the case with the Amish.

The geographic and cultural setting of the case was significant. The cheese-making Swiss-Americans of the New Glarus community were less than enthusiastic about the Amish settling in their community. The local school administrators were ambitious in promoting the educational standards of Wisconsin. The State Department of Education was daring enough to appeal the case to the Supreme Court in Washington. The latter is important. Wisconsin, not the Amish, pushed the case to the U.S. Supreme Court. The Amish were not the aggressors in a suit of law.

The New Glarus Amish community was a small one. This fact made it easier for the National Committee for Amish Religious Freedom to get the needed cooperation and consent of the Amish parents to appeal the case to higher courts. The bishops overseeing the New Glarus community did not prevent the defendants from giving their consent to the National Committee. We know of at least one bishop in another state who expressed trepidation about taking the issue to higher courts.[2] The Amish are extremely careful and usually reluctant to permit others to litigate in their behalf.

When the Amish refused to pay self-employment tax for Old Age and Survivors Insurance (Social Security) and the IRS took away their horses, attorney Shepard Cole came to their legal defense. After Cole had completed all the necessary legal work, the Amish bishops changed their minds as they ascended the steps of the Federal District Court and decided not to contest the case. In the Wisconsin case this situation was avoided.

THE RELIGIOUS FACTOR

The Amish have suffered repeatedly at the hands of school officials who have not understood their concern for education, or the distinction they make between technology and wisdom, between the critical analytical method and the quest for social coherence in their community life. Most law enforcement officials and school administrators have not understood the religious issue.

When in 1965 the Iowa Amish refused to send their children to the consolidated public school, the state and county officials asserted that the Amish objections were economic rather than religious. From the attorney general's office to local board members, public officials held that the Amish wanted to avoid the expense of hiring certified teachers. Neighbors of the Amish told state officials that religious conviction was not involved in the question of certification. They pointed to the fact that the Amish families had for fourteen years used certified teachers in their schools. But what was taken by the non-Amish community to be stubbornness, noncooperation, and a parsimonious attitude toward education was for the Amish leaders a central religious principle with a background of over two centuries of experience. The Amish sensed intuitively what scientists know empirically, that when a secular system of education displaces the indigenous method of training, the basis for a traditional way of life is swept away.

Five cultural themes in Amish society have significant implications for socialization: separation from the world; voluntary acceptance of high social obligations, symbolized by adult baptism; maintenance of a disciplined church-community; practices of exclusion and shunning of transgressing members; and a life in harmony with the soil and nature.[3] Since socialization and therefore also schooling are directly related to the underlying themes of a culture, it is important to understand the basic beliefs of Amish society at the outset.

Separation From the World

Two biblical passages, perhaps the most often quoted, epitomize for the Amishman the message of separation. The first is: "Be not conformed to this world, but be ye transformed by the renewing of your mind that ye may prove what is that good and acceptable and perfect will of God" (Romans 12:1). It is the duty of a Christian to keep himself "unspotted from the world" and separate from the desires, intent, and goals of the worldly person. To the Amishman this means, among other things, that one should not dress and behave like the world. Another key passage is "Be ye not unequally yoked together with unbelievers; for what fellowship hath righteousness with unrighteousness? and what communion hath light with darkness?" (II Corinthians 6:14). The church, according to biblical teaching, must be "pure," "without blemish," and "without spot or wrinkle." These teachings forbid the Amishman from marrying a non-Amish person or from entering into a business partnership with an outsider. The doctrine applies to all social contacts that would involve intimate connections with persons outside the ceremonial community. The emphasis on separation has given rise to a view of themselves as a "chosen people" or "peculiar people."

The Amish are forbidden by the precepts and example of Christ to take part in violence and war. When drafted for military service, they apply for conscientious objector status, basing their stand on biblical texts such as "My kingdom is not of this world: if my kingdom were of this world, then would my servants fight" (John 18:36). The Amish find no biblical rationale for self-defense. Like many early Anabaptists they are "defenseless Christians." Problems of hostility are met with no retaliation. The Amish farmer, in difficulty with the hostile world around him, is admonished by his bishop to follow the biblical example of Isaac. After the warring Philistines had stopped up all the wells of his father Abraham, Isaac moved to new lands and dug new wells (Genesis 26:15-18). The Amish take this advice literally, so that in the face of hostility, they move to new locations without defending their civil or legal rights. When confronted with school consolidation that makes it impossible to remain separate from the world, they build private schools or migrate to another county, state, or country.

Although the Amish maintain separation from the world, they are not highly ethnocentric in their personal relations with non-Amish persons. They accept as a matter of course other persons as they are, without attempting to judge them or convert them to the Amish way of life. For those who are born and reared in Amish society, however, the sanctions for belonging to the group are deeply rooted in the belief in separation from the world as defined by the church-community.

Voluntary Acceptance of High Social Obligations, Symbolized by Adult Baptism

The meaning of baptism to the individual and to the community reflects an important core value. Basic to the baptismal vow is the acknowledgment of Christ as the Son of God, belief in the spiritual sovereignty of the true church of God on earth, the "renunciation of the world, the devil, one's own flesh and blood, and confession of Christ as Lord and Savior." The formal confession is no different from many other Christian groups. What is significant is the promise to abide by the Ordnung and the promise "not to depart from the discipline in life or death."

Great emphasis is placed on walking the "straight and narrow way." Voluntary membership is emphasized, but for one who has been baptized there is no turning back. In support of the religious beliefs an Amish preacher told the court, "We don't go down on our knees for nothing." Applicants are warned not to make a promise they cannot keep.

The Maintenance of a Disciplined Church-Community

The Amish community is distinct from other church groups in that most of the rules governing life are not specified in writing. These values and norms can be known only by being a participant. The rules for living tend to form a body of sentiments that are essential to the practice of true Christian brotherhood.

All Amish members know the Ordnung of their church district. Because most rules are taken for granted, it is usually those questionable or borderline issues that are specified in the

Ordnung. These rules are reviewed at a special service preceding
communion Sunday. They must have been unanimously endorsed
by the ministers. At the members' meeting following the regular
service they are presented orally, after which members are asked
to give assent to the Ordnung. Members must be able to say
individually that they are at peace with all other members.
Without this essential unity the communion service cannot be
observed.

Excommunication and Shunning ("Bann und Meidung")

These are the church-community's means of dealing with
obdurate and erring members and of keeping the church pure.
The doctrine was intrinsic to the Anabaptist movement from its
very beginning. The Anabaptist concept of the church was of
a pure church consisting of believers only; persons who violate
the discipline must first be excommunicated, then shunned.
This method of dealing with offenders, the Amish say, is
taught by Christ (Matthew 18:15-17), and the Apostle Paul
explains (I Corinthians 5:11) that members must not keep
company with unrepentant members nor eat with them.
The passage is interpreted to mean that a person who has broken
his vow with God and who will not mend his ways must be
expelled from the fellowship just as the human body casts off
an infectious growth. The practice of shunning among the
Swiss Mennonites was to exclude the offender from communion.
A more emphatic practice was advanced by Jacob Amman.
His interpretation required shunning excommunicated persons
not only at communion but also in social and economic life.
Shunning means that members may receive no favors from an
excommunicated person, that they may not buy from nor
sell to an excommunicated person, and that no member shall
eat at the same table with an excommunicated person.

The ban is used as an instrument of discipline not only
for the drunkard or the adulterer, but for the person who
transgresses the discipline of the church. Parents, for example,
who send their children to a school beyond that required
for living in the Amish community are liable for censure.

The same applies to any member who obtains a worldly education.

Life Close to the Soil and Nature

Implicit in Amish culture is the view that nature is a garden, that man was made to be a caretaker (not an exploiter) in the garden, and that manual labor is good. The physical world is viewed as good and not in itself corrupting or evil. The beauty in the universe is perceived in the orderliness of the seasons, the grandeur of the heavens, the intricate world of growing plants, the diversity of animals, and the forces of living and dying.

The preference for rural living is reflected in attitudes and informal relations for group life, rather than in an explicit dogma. The Amish believe that God is pleased when man works in harmony with nature, the soil, and the weather, and cares for plants and animals. Hard work, thrift, and mutual aid are virtues upheld in the Bible. The city, by contrast, is viewed by the Amish as the center of leisure, nonproductive spending, and often wickedness. The Christian life, they content, is best maintained away from cities. God created Adam and Eve to "replenish the earth, and subdue it; and have dominion over the fish of the sea, and over the fowl of the air, and over every living thing that moveth upon the earth" (Genesis 1:28). Man's highest place in the universe is to care for the things of creation.

These five cultural themes play an important part in the education of the young. Complete separation is not a goal nor do the Amish think of themselves as better than other people. Wholeness and separation are not considered antithetical, but complementary for the continued existence of a prized way of life. Like parents in any society, the Amish want their children to absorb the basic values of their way of life. Many Amish fear the loss of their cohesive spiritual tradition. Their concern is not simply that their children may become "English," but that they may be lost for eternity. Inability to teach their children the Amish way of life affects the parents' relation to God, the community, and themselves. Parents are accountable to God for rearing their children in the faith and to fail to do this is to leave a blemish on the church. To lose one's children to the world is to lose hope of spending eternity with them in heaven.

EDUCATIONAL GOALS

True education, according to the Amish, is "the cultivation of humility, simple living, and resignation to the will of God." For generations the Amish have centered instruction in reading, writing, arithmetic, and the moral teachings of the Bible. They stress training for life participation (here and for eternity) and warn of the perils of "pagan" philosophy and the intellectual enterprises of "fallen man," as did their forefathers.[4] Historically, the Anabaptist avoided all training associated with self-exaltation, pride of position, enjoyment of power, and the arts of war and violence. Memorization, recitation, and personal relationships between teacher and pupil were part of a system of education that was supremely social and communal.

Growing up in a separated society is different from growing up in a mainstream denomination in the United States. In a denomination much of the larger society is affirmed and public education may differ little from the culture of established religions. However, if the Amish child is removed from his community and put into the consolidated school in the larger society, there is sharp discontinuity for him. In the Amish school such arbitrary distinctions between school and life do not exist, for the primary function of the Amish school is not education in the narrow sense of instruction but the creation of a learning environment continuous with Amish culture. By identifying with teachers who identify with them, children acquire understanding essential to becoming an adult. The Amish school atmosphere supports the values and attitudes of the separated community, and the individual is socialized to develop his skills and personality within the small community. Emphasis is on interaction and continuity of lives; of teachers with pupils and of parents with children.

THE FACE-TO-FACE COMMUNITY IN JEOPARDY

The Amish are opposed to separating school from life. The highest form of religious life is, for them, brotherhood or self-realization of community life. When this is undermined, the religious life is threatened. The Amish are opposed to schools that undermine the spiritual basis of community life.

When the population in the United States was primarily rural and the major occupation was farming, the Amish people had no real objections to public schooling. Some mixing with "English" or non-Amish children is still considered desirable by many Amish parents. In the traditional country school the Amish child received a little contact with other children. In the rural public school the Amish child was treated as a member of a group rather than as a unique personality. The songs learned were largely religious; they were copied into notebooks and sung in unison, as is done in the Amish tradition. The Amish children achieved their basic skills in reading, writing, and arithmetic, and the school was acceptable to the Amish, even though a considerable portion of the program was neither meaningful nor relevant to the Amish way of life. The method of learning (by oral means and by example) was consistent with the Amish culture. So long as the schools were small and near their farm homes, the Amish were able to moderate exposure to alien values. With public school consolidation these conditions changed.

The Amish community requires face-to-face contacts in order to remain viable. Its cohesiveness is based upon personal responsibility and shared values. The primary unit remains small and on a human rather than an organizational scale. As long as the public school maintained this human scale, the Amish were satisfied, and many were active participants in the schools.

The Amish struggle to maintain the school on a human rather than an organizational scale has centered on four major issues:

• *The location of the school.* The Amish insist that their children attend schools located close to their homes in an agricultural environment, so that children can help with the farm work and aspire to become farmers, for farming is a basic tenet in the Amish way of life. Consolidation threatens the homogeneous character of the Amish community and exposes the children to alien values. To avoid these perils the Amish founded one- and two-room private schools.

> • *The training and qualifications of the teacher.* In order to teach their way of life, the Amish want to have qualified teachers committed to Amish values. Their method of teaching is largely based on example and learning by doing. Persons qualified by state standards are incapable of teaching the Amish way of life by the example of their lives.

> • *The number of years of schooling.* The Amish want their children educated in the basic skills of reading, writing, and arithmetic in elementary school. All training beyond that, they say, should be conducive to the Amish religion and way of life. Conflict developed over the number of years of schooling when states raised the age requirement from 14 to 16 and in some instances to 18 years.

> • *The content of education.* The Amish basically object to having their children trained for a way of life that is contrary to their religion. "Public or free schools," they say, "are intended only to impart worldly knowledge, to insure earthly success, and to make good citizens for the state." The Amish say it is the duty of the church-community to prepare their children to live spiritually in this life and for eternity.

The alternatives confronting the Amish were these: permit the children to attend the large schools (more liberalized groups have done so), request officials to keep the one-room school open, vote down the consolidation option and higher taxes, ignore compulsory attendance laws after the completion of eighth grade, or open private schools of their own. The Old Order Amish, who have no training in either secondary schools or college, responded to the challenge by building and staffing their own schools. Their schools originated in response to state consolidation of public schools in this country. The first Amish school was built in 1925. In 1950 there were 16 schools and in 1970 over 300, with an estimated enrollment of 10,000 pupils.

✟ Of six main arguments in favor of school consolidation, none are acceptable to the Amish:[5]

• "Equalization of costs between the poorer and wealthier districts." The Amish do not care if their district is financially poor, for simplicity and modesty are considered virtues.

• "Better teachers." The Amish do not believe that higher education necessarily produces better teachers, nor that higher salaries insure greater competence.

• "Superior curricula." The Amish consider the curriculum of the larger schools inferior, for it usually stresses science and lauds technology.

• "Specialization of instruction and grading of pupils by age groups." The Amish are opposed to specialized instruction, preferring that their children learn only the basic skills of reading, writing, and arithmetic. They consider it a disadvantage to group children only with their age-mates rather than letting them associate in a mixed group, where the younger children can learn from the older and the older children can help the younger.

• "Social advantages to pupils and to the community." This is considered a danger rather than an advantage, because the Amish wish their children to follow in their own footsteps and not to move on to other occupations or higher-status jobs.

• "Better administration and superior vision." The Amish are suspicious of administration, for they believe that agreements should be informal and based on the word of the parties concerned. There is little need for administration in small face-to-face groups. The Amish also believe the vision of administrative officials to be inferior rather than superior, for it is usually progress-oriented and based on an exclusive belief in the scientific method.

EDUCATIONAL ACHIEVEMENT

In our study of Amish culture, personality, and achievement patterns, we found little evidence of alienation or human deprivation.[6] As judged by educational testing standards the overall performance of the Amish is similar to that of a representative sample of rural school children in the United States. In spite of the limited exposure (the Amish children have no radio, television, and modern school facilities), and although the

Amish teachers themselves have had only an eighth-grade
education, Amish pupils scored significantly higher in spelling,
word usage, and arithmetic than the pupils in our sample of
rural public schools. They scored slightly above the national norm
in these subjects in spite of small libraries and limited equipment.
The Amish pupils were equal to the non-Amish pupils in
reading comprehension and in the use of reference material.
They scored lowest in vocabulary. In those aspects of learning
stressed by the Amish culture, the Amish pupils outdid pupils
in the control group.

The Amish culture provides an environment for its children
that is rather sharply delineated from the social climate of our
western civilization. By outside standards this environment is
limiting and restricting, but to the Amish child it provides
reasonable fulfillment and a knowledge of what is expected
of him. Learning is directed toward conformity with a knowledge
of what is right, rather than toward questioning existing
knowledge or discovering new knowledge. Any effort to increase
creativity or raise performance on standardized school tests among
the Amish cannot be undertaken without also introducing the
risk of cultural discontinuities. The introduction of greater
competitive goals, resulting in greater appeal to self-interest and
to self-importance, can only mean in Amish terms the loss of
"humility, simple living, and resignation to the will of God."

The Amish personality type may be described as quiet,
responsible, and conscientious.[7] The Amishman works devotedly
to meet his obligations, and although careful with detail,
he needs time to master technical subjects. He is not especially
good at working rapidly with complicated tasks. He likes to do
things well. The Amish modal personality is loyal, considerate,
sympathetic. The Amishman is concerned with how other people
feel, even when they are in the wrong. He dislikes telling people
unpleasant things. These personality endowments correspond
generally with the values stressed in Amish culture.

Amish children tend to be very aware of other people,
they prefer a certain amount of routine, and they relate well
to most people. Their drawings reveal preferences for work-related
activities; they do not make a sharp distinction between what is

work and what is play. Happy-time activities reveal no rigid differentiation between the sexes. Drawings of the Amish home, as the children see it, include a variety of colors, often several buildings, and a spatial orientation of the farm environment that includes roads, gardens, and fences. The drawings reveal a realistic sense of environment, an ability to conceptualize space at an early age, and a strong identification of the individual with the home. The inclusion of others in their drawings suggests the importance of family and group activities.

The vocational preferences of Amish children are for service occupations and manual work. The children emulate the work roles of adults. Amish boys generally prefer farming or farm-related work. Girls prefer housekeeping, gardening, cooking, cleaning, caring for children, or some type of service, such as nursing or teaching. Their vocational aspirations are realistic and attainable within the limits of Amish culture.

CULTURAL PLURALISM IS VIABLE

The Amish grounding is firmly religious. In addition, the sociology of Amish life is also credible in that it works. There are, however, several significant elements in the larger American culture favorable to the Amish plight. At present the relationship between education and religion is in flux. Both education and religion are undergoing major changes and jarring transitions. Religion is attempting to cope with rapid social change. The growing competition between the major world religions, the secularization of most industrial societies, the elimination of mystery through scientific enquiry—all of these are unsettling to religion. In most societies religion has functioned as an anchor of the basic values. In fact, that is the way religion functions in Amish society. In contemporary American society the complexity of the social order has resulted in separating religion and moral values.

The question of religious training in a pluralistic society is a thorny one. In this connection, there is a real danger that education in American society may itself become a religion. Furthermore, if, as a society, we rely on the values which safeguard pluralism, but do not nurture the affirmations in which they are anchored, we have no evidence that pluralism will continue to be a viable reality. American commitments to pluralism and to secular education are in some sense contradictory and will continue to be so. There is much evidence that public policy in terms of minority groups and culturally different children has made no recent significant gains. The public schools have not promoted pluralism. The melting pot theory may have functioned well when there was need to establish identity as a nation. Today the situation is different. What people want and feel they need is self-identity and community realization. When culturally different children attend a school that teaches an unattainable identity—an identity that would demand the rejection of values of the home, tribe, or street, or even skin color— only alienation and rebellion can be expected.

Examples of abuses on this level committed against children are legion. In New York City teachers are known to lecture Puerto Rican students on how rude it is to speak a "strange" language in the presence of those who do not understand it.[8] In the Southwest, where it is widely believed that a child's native language "holds him back," children are threatened, shamed, and punished for speaking the only language they know. Humiliated for their language and values, they are forced to endure the teaching of a culture unrelated to the realities of their lives, and it is no wonder that children withdraw mentally and are uninterested in going to school.

If learning is to be relevant, then teachers must pay far more attention to the cultural context of the children they teach. A vivid illustration of this was an encounter between Benjamin Franklin and the Delaware Indians in 1744. Franklin observed that at Williamsburg there was a college with a fund for educating Indian young people. He invited the chiefs to send a half dozen of their sons to the college. The government, he said, would see that they were well provided for and instructed in all the learning of the white people.

The Indian spokesman replied: "We know that you highly esteem the kind of learning taught in your schools, and that you mean to do us good by your proposal, and we thank you heartily. But you who are wise must know that different nations have

different conceptions of things, and that you will not take it
amiss, if our ideas of this kind of education happen not to be
the same as yours. We have had some experience with it.
Several of our young people were formerly brought up at the
colleges of the northern provinces. They were instructed in all
your sciences, but when they came back to us they were bad
runners, ignorant of every means of living in the woods,
unable to bear cold or hunger, knew neither how to build a cabin,
take a deer, nor kill an enemy, spoke our language imperfectly,
and were therefore neither fit for hunters, warriors or councillors.
They were totally good for nothing."[9]

The court's decision on the Wisconsin Amish is a reminder
of how far all Americans have departed from basic commitments
to pluralism and the willingness to permit differences to exist
side by side in an atmosphere of religious liberty. Every profession
should regulate its own excesses, and in the absence of that,
we can be grateful for a Supreme Court that restrains the
state departments of education from destroying the very
foundation of good intergroup relations in our society.

7

Building a Landmark Case: *Wisconsin* v *Yoder*

William B. Ball

William B. Ball, an attorney in Harrisburg, Pennsylvania, has argued numerous church-state cases. He conducted the three-year defense of the Wisconsin Amish, culminating in the U.S. Supreme Court decision of May 15, 1972.

In "Building a Landmark Case" he describes the process of litigation as the case moved through the various stages of appeal and defense.

On Christmas Eve, 1968, I received a call from the Reverend William Lindholm, Chairman of the National Committee for Amish Religious Freedom. He told me that Amish parents in Wisconsin had been arrested under a criminal complaint for refusal to enroll their children in high school. I subsequently told the Reverend Mr. Lindholm that I thought the matter was one that could be readily resolved—that we ought to write to the Superintendent of Public Instruction of the State of Wisconsin, informing him of what I now know to be true: that there was some daylight in their compulsory attendance statute whereby these Amish children could be exempted from high school attendance.

Accordingly, we wrote the superintendent, being very careful to make him understand that the National Committee for Amish Religious Freedom was not a national test-casing pressure group. As a handful of scholars and lawyers and religious leaders, we looked sympathetically at the plight of the Amish people, and we believed that we had found a solution useful to Wisconsin in its problem with these people. We then pointed out how the children in question could be exempted under the law.

It seemed to be the part of common sense that they should be. If the law allowed for it, why put Wisconsin to the expense of a trial? Why subject the Amish to the burden of a criminal proceeding? Then occurred the first major surprise which Wisconsin was to afford us in this case: a short reply that exemption could not be granted, followed by what we felt were totally insupportable reasons. Thus it was apparent that a trial was going to be inevitable. Preparation for it began immediately.

What did we have to go on? The Amish had previously been in court on the schooling question in several states. How had those courts ruled? Unfortunately, adversely. The decision of the Superior Court of Pennsylvania on this point said that there was no constitutional basis for declaring them exempt from attendance at high school. There was a similar decision from the courts of Ohio and, more recently, *State* v. *Garber*, in which the Supreme Court of Kansas ruled against the Amish. That decision was especially adverse because it had been appealed to the Supreme Court of the United States, and the Court had refused review. This indicated that, in the mind of the highest Court of the land, refusal of the Amish to send their children to high school did not present any significant constitutional issue of religious liberty.

So we had no precedent cases on our side to go on. Our solace at the moment might have been found in a statement of Jonathan Swift:

> It is a maxim among lawyers that whatever hath been done before may legally be done again, and therefore the lawyers take special care to record all the decisions formerly made against common justice and the general reason of mankind.

In searching for precedent, we did, however, find one golden nugget we thought we could seize upon. That was the decision of the U.S. Supreme Court in *Sherbert* v. *Verner*, which involved the following. In South Carolina, in the early 1960s, a woman named Adele Sherbert applied for unemployment compensation. The State Board of Unemployment Compensation turned her down, stating that she had been offered employment and had refused it. She, however, said the employment offered her had called for work on Saturdays. As a Seventh Day Adventist, she could not work on Saturday. The board denied her plea, and she took an appeal into the courts and up to the Supreme Court of South Carolina, where she lost. She then appealed to the Supreme Court of the United States, which reversed the decision on the ground of violation of her religious liberty. It said that religious liberty is a highly protected freedom under our constitution. It is not an absolute liberty, but if the state violates anybody's religious liberty, it may only do so in the name of a "compelling state interest."

The Court, in *Sherbert*, of course recognized that the unemployment compensation system constitutes a "compelling state interest." When may a "compelling state interest" override religious liberty? The Court said, in effect, only when that legitimate interest is really threatened: "Only the gravest abuses, endangering paramount interests, give occasion for permissible limitation." In other words, the exercise of one's religion must pose a real threat to some major interest which the state has a right to protect, before the state may curtail that exercise. If a person sacrifices human beings in his back yard as a part of his religion, he is obviously confronting the interest of the state in protecting human life. The state may limit him in this exercise of his religion.

The kinds of cases the courts have recognized as presenting situations in which religious liberty can be limited are cases which offend general public policy in an extreme way— for example, polygamy. The Supreme Court, in 1878, ruled that the Mormons might enjoy their religion, but not in its full implications. In other words, Mormons may not practice polygamy because it threatens the very heart of society.

We looked then at *Sherbert* v. *Verner* with its tests of
"compelling state interest" and actuality of threat to that interest,
and believed that here lay the basic constitutional theory on which
our Amish case would have to rest. It is true that *Sherbert* was not
a case involving education, parents, or the commission of a crime.
Adele Sherbert was not involved with any criminal statute.
Our clients in Wisconsin were.

If we were going to succeed in the case, we would have to
structure it carefully. First of all, we would show that there was a
true religious liberty claim involved—that we were not dealing
with some "instant," overnight religion. We would have to prove
that the Amish religion does have binding effects upon its
members; that it is real, and their belief is sincere. Furthermore,
we would have to show that the state was violating the practice
of this religion by the Amish people. We would also have to show
that no compelling state interest was involved, and the action of
the Amish in keeping their children out of high school did not
present any significant threat to that compelling state interest—
an interest which the state certainly has in education.

We came to trial in March of 1969, in the Green County,
Wisconsin, court house, a quaint little place well outfitted with
brass spittoons. A considerate and pleasant judge was on the bench.
We decided, first of all, to put on the stand the local school
superintendent who had doubled as the truant officer. We
introduced the point that he had arrested the defendants
immediately after the Amish had set up a little elementary
parochial school, which had the effect of depriving the local
school district of $18,000 of state subsidy. Turning from
cross-examination, we were now able to put on our own
affirmative cause.

We began by putting on the record the nature of the Amish
religion. Here we were blessed with the most superb witness we
could have had, Dr. John Hostetler, an authority on the Amish
people. We wanted to bring out why these Amish children
could not go to high school and yet could go to grade school.
We needed to underscore the significance of adolescence and
adult baptism in the Amish religion and tradition. We had to
establish the certainty of Amish belief—that it isn't something

one flips a coin about, but that it has a certainty and force of
command for its members.

There followed one of the most interesting exchanges
during three years of litigation. Dr. Hostetler was taken under
fire in cross-examination by the state prosecutor who had his
own ideas about education.

The Prosecutor: "Now, Doctor, let's talk about education.
What's the point of education? Isn't it to get ahead in the world?"

Dr. Hostetler's superb answer: "It all depends on which
world." That is the most beautiful piece of testimony I have
ever heard.

We also wanted to give the state an opportunity to
cross-examine Amish witnesses. We put on the stand an Amish girl
who had stayed away from school; the Reverend Mr. Hershberger,
an Amish minister; and one of the defendant parents, Wallace
Miller. There is great truth in a statement in the Bible about the
wisdom of the simple: the prosecutor could not confound these
witnesses. In fact, he had a tough problem: he could put them
through a long cross-examination to bring out his case,
get them to contradict themselves, and confuse them. But if he
took that route (because he had sampled enough of their answers
and their demeanor on the stand), he knew he would appear
foolish to hound them. So he let them go. Later, we were able
to say repeatedly to the courts as we went up on appeal,
that with every opportunity to cross-examine these witnesses,
the state never made its case with respect to them.

Next, we needed to look at the "compelling state interest"
and whether the Amish people, by abstention from high school,
were presenting a significant threat to that interest.

We began by putting on the stand the people who might
best know about this. For example, the local sheriff. We asked
him the usual foundation questions: "Do you know the Amish
in this community?, Are you familiar with them?, Do you know
Amish youngsters when you see them?," and so forth. His answers
were all in the affirmative.

Then we went on with: "How many of these Amish of
high-school age or older have committed crimes of looting, arson,

rape, theft, drunken driving, etc.?" His answers were all in the negative.

Then we put the county director of welfare on the stand. We asked him: "How many Amish are in state homes for the aged?, How many are in state homes for alcoholics?, How many are on welfare?, Is any threat to the state posed by Amish ways in education?"

We then called to the stand, as an expert witness, Professor Donald Erickson of the University of Chicago, who has done important writing in the field of education. We questioned him at some length on the meaning of "education." The state was saying that the Amish children were being deprived of an "education." What is "education"?

Professor Erickson was asked this question: "The state compulsory attendance law gives Amish people three apparent courses to take: (a) to establish their own parochial school (which they refuse to do) (b) to place their children in public high school (c) to refuse to do both of these and suffer the penalties of the law unless the courts decide that their constitutional liberty is violated. Leaving the last point aside, as a professional educator, what sort of choice do you think this is?"

His answer: "I don't think it's any choice at all. Educationally, I have never seen a school that has impressed me either as a culturally or religiously neutral school. Should minority groups be permitted to decide whether or not they should be educated? Answer: My first reaction is that it is a false question. There is no such thing as a noneducation. Every child is educated through the process of child socialization. The best way is to have some group determining what education is to be given to particular children."

He went on to say that the Amish children were in a fortunate position of being able to learn by doing, an ideal system of education: "I think that we are learning more and more that the current educational system is detached from the real world. They talk about things that the children don't become involved in and toward which they have no sense of responsibility. There is a clear lack of connection between learning and doing in most of our education which is responsible for much of our student actions and some of the troubles we have today."

The defendants were found guilty. The court acknowledged that their religious liberty had been violated but said there was a superior state interest in forcing the children to attend school.

We took an appeal immediately to the District Court, the intermediate appellate court in Wisconsin. We lost again. Then we took an appeal to the Supreme Court of Wisconsin, which, in a splendid opinion, reversed the lower courts and held that the Amish children should be exempt:

> The Amish children would experience a useless anguish of living in two worlds. Either the public school is irrelevant in their lives as members of the Old Order Amish community or these secondary school values will make all future life as Amish impossible to them.

Now, we came to the second big surprise of the case. The state sent us word that it was appealing the case to the Supreme Court of the United States. It was going to drag the Amish to Washington. We greeted that with absolute disbelief. We could not imagine why the state wanted to pursue this baseless prosecution any further, having received so decisive an answer by the Wisconsin Supreme Court.

The Supreme Court of the United States was then faced with the question of whether or not to hear the case. In *Kansas* v. *Garber*, a few years before, the Court had refused to hear a similar case involving the Amish. Now it agreed to review. We wondered whether, in acceding to Wisconsin's request, the Court was not indicating its sympathy with Wisconsin's position. On December 8, 1971, oral argument in the case took place. On May 15, 1972, the Court decided in favor of the Amish people. A great crossing had been made in religious liberty in this country.

I want to conclude by mentioning briefly a few points relating to the case. First, there is inherent in this case a question of the *definition of religion*. In its opinion, the Court recognized that the Amish have sincere and understandable beliefs. But the

State of Wisconsin, in its brief before the Court, pressed this one point insistently: "The Amish are free to worship as they please. Therefore, how can anyone say their religious liberty is being violated?" The notion of confining religion by defining religion, of saying that religion is what the state says it is, was a serious point to be contended with in Wisconsin's position. Wisconsin was saying that religion is worship—and that is all. The circumscription of religion which the State of Wisconsin insisted upon is a dangerous doctrine. It makes the right of worship completely equal to a right of religious liberty. This concept would destroy the Amish religion, which is communal in nature. One cannot become Amish by attending some church or signing up as a member. Amish daily life is permeated with concepts of religious relationships. Religion is the community and the community is religion. Wisconsin's argument is really that of the *Kulturkampf* of Bismarck: keep religion within the sacristy, within the church meeting house; that is the outer limit of religious liberty.

Another point of special interest in the case is the dichotomy between freedom to believe and freedom to act. The state insisted that religious liberty consists simply of a freedom to believe. Of course the courts have not recognized that religious liberty is limited simply to freedom to believe, and here certainly the Supreme Court did not.

A third interesting aspect relates to the role of religion in public education. Professor Robert Ulich of Harvard in a book he coauthored with Professor Paul Freund, also of Harvard, entitled *Religion in Public Education*, speaks of the mission of the public school teacher as being "to educate freely minds which on one hand appreciate the depth of man's religious tradition of the past but to whom on the other, the old denominational, dualistic conflicts appear secondary if not inhibitive to the formation of a unifying world outlook." Here is really a religious judgment. Education, say these authors, is to be "above the warrings of the denominations" and should pronounce judgments on these. But we must not forget that the contentions of the denominations are contentions for religious truths. By the

Ulich-Freund prescription, the public educator is in fact to decide
what is true and what is false in religious matters.

Today we have in our public schools a strong prescription
against any teaching of religion. This came about because of cases,
such as *Engle* and *Schempp*, in which Jewish children and some
children of other religions complained about the presence of
Bible reading and the Lord's Prayer in the schools. There was some
good sense in the Supreme Court's ruling that the public school
must not be an agent for imposing religious beliefs and practices
on children. But let us take the case of a boy who is raised, say,
in the Church of the Nazarene. He is taught to believe that the
Bible is true, that the Bible is the Word of God. When that child
today is placed in a public school environment in which the Bible
is not referred to as the Word of God, there arises, I think,
a serious problem of religious liberty because such a child is not
readily able to maintain his religious faith in an environment
in which the central belief of his religion is treated by his teachers
as not necessarily true, or with indifferent "neutrality."

Again, the *Yoder* case relates to parental rights and to the
definition of education to which we have already referred.
Further, it relates to the question of technology. Franklin Littel,
the great Protestant author of *From State Church to Pluralism*,
spoke, at a meeting in Chicago, of our contemporary education
which so completely emphasizes science and technology. Littel
said that it emphasizes the "how" as opposed to the "why."
It fails to emphasize questions like, "Who am I?" and "Where am
I going?" Instead it emphasizes "How do you do this? How is
this made? How to improve interrelations in groups? How?"
This tremendous emphasis on "how," supplanting the emphasis
on "why," presents a serious problem for people today who are
trying to become "educated" but might wish to come to learn
the ways of God.

The Amish reject (which some may feel is extreme)
"higher learning" and scientific learning. But what they have
instead, I believe, is wisdom—a wisdom which I think is speaking
to us in our time.

My experience with the Amish case leaves me in their debt
because of what these good people have taught me. I think the

whole country has a great deal to thank the Amish and Mennonite people for. We should thank them for their great contributions to the cause of religious freedom.

8

Compulsory Education: The Plain People Resist

Stephen Arons

A lawyer and teacher at the University of Massachusetts, Amherst, Stephen Arons frequently writes on legal questions relating to education, and is one of the authors of *Doing Your Own School* (Boston: Beacon Press, 1973).

In this article, written several months before the U.S. Supreme Court handed down its decision, Arons observes that while the legal question in the Wisconsin case is quite narrow—May Amish children be exempted from compulsory education?—its implications are broad and far-reaching, for the case calls into question whether a state establishment of values does not, in fact, like state establishment of religion, violate some of the basic tenets of the Bill of Rights.

In September of 1968, Jonas Yoder and two other Amish residents of Wisconsin refused, because of their religious beliefs, to send their children to high school. In so doing, they exposed themselves to criminal prosecution and possible prison sentences for defying the state's compulsory attendance law. In December 1971, the United States Supreme Court heard oral arguments on whether or not Wisconsin may constitutionally limit the free exercise of religion by means of a compulsory school law aimed in effect at inculcating majority-approved "secular" values in the minds of dissenters. In their simple act of conscience, the Amish defendants raised another major issue in the conflict between state power and individual freedom. (Amish residents in a number of states have repeatedly been fined or jailed for refusing to obey compulsory attendance laws, but this is the first time the issue has reached the Supreme Court.)

The legal question involved in this case, though it is among the most important religious freedom issues ever heard by the Court, is quite narrow. A lower state court tried and convicted the Amish parents. The Wisconsin Supreme Court reversed the convictions and exempted Amish children above the eighth grade from the compulsory school law because it violates their religious prohibition against formal education. But the law remains intact as applied to everyone else, and both parties in the case have been at pains to insist that no general challenge to compulsory education is presented by the exemption.

The narrowness of this legal decision should not, however, obscure its far-reaching implications for public policy. The case does, in fact, call into question the entire rationale for compulsory schooling. *Wisconsin* v. *Yoder* confronts us with the fact that state establishment of values, like the establishment of religion, is a threat to the tenets set down by the Bill of Rights.

When the first Amish migrated to America from Switzerland in the late seventeenth century, they were in search of religious freedom. When, nearly 250 years later, they were brought to criminal trial in Wisconsin on a complaint filed by the New Glarus public school administrator, they were still searching for religious freedom. . . .

No one denies that the compulsory attendance law interferes with Amish religious practices and beliefs. In supporting this conclusion, both the trial court and the Wisconsin Supreme Court rejected the state's claim that actions and beliefs are separable for the Amish. There is no serious disagreement with the contention by the defense's expert witness, Dr. John Hostetler, author of *Amish Society*, that the imposition on Amish youth of

the value system of high school will result in psychological
alienation of the child and destruction of the Amish faith-
community. In spite of this, the trial court convicted the
defendants for having violated the compulsory school attendance
law.

The court convicted these dissenters from the technological
mainstream because it found that the imposition on the Amish
was justified by the state's "reasonable" interest in uniform
compulsory attendance. To put this finding in its starkest light,
the trial court seems to have believed that in choosing between
two views of the route to salvation—one called religious practice
and the other called compulsory school attendance—the state's
version should prevail.

In balancing the burden borne by the Amish against the
interest of the state in uniform compulsory attendance, however,
the legal presumption favors the Amish. When First Amendment
rights such as the free exercise of religion are involved, the state
must justify infringements, not simply by reference to a reasonable
purpose it holds, but by defining a "compelling" state interest,
one so important that not pursuing it would create a clear danger
to society. It was for the absence of such a compelling interest
that the Wisconsin Supreme Court reversed the convictions and
declared the compulsory attendance law unconstitutional as
applied to the Amish. The court noted: "To the Amish, secondary
schools not only teach an unacceptable value system, but they
also seek to integrate ethnic groups into a homogenized society . . ."
and as a result ". . . the education they receive in public school
is irrelevant to their lives . . . or will make life as Amish
impossible." The court could find no compelling state interest
sufficient to warrant this effect, especially in view of the fact
that an exemption for the Amish left the compulsory attendance
law in effect for all others.

Following this ruling, the state Attorney General's office
took up the cudgel and asked the U.S. Supreme Court for a
hearing. If the Supreme Court affirms the decision, it will
strengthen the view that it is not the state but the parents who
hold the right to direct the upbringing of children according to
their own views, at least when these are sincerely held religious

beliefs. Up to this point the strongest legal support for this position came from *Pierce* v. *Society of Sisters*, a 1925 case in which a Ku Klux Klan-supported Oregon law requiring children to attend only public schools was held unconstitutional. In so doing, the Court said: "The fundamental theory of liberty upon which all governments in the Union repose excludes any general power of the State to standardize its children by forcing them to accept instruction from public teachers only."

In his dissent in the Wisconsin case, one Justice sought to avoid going beyond the *Pierce* affirmation of a choice among private and public schools. Justice Heffernan reasoned that, although the values of the public high school may indeed be repugnant to the Amish religion, the Amish may establish private schools, thereby satisfying the state's interest in compulsory attendance while preserving the right of Amish parents to direct the upbringing of their children. This proposed resolution, however, misunderstands the Amish community. It is not simply public school to which they object, but *all* schooling above the eighth grade. The dissent implies that the Amish practice of education through experience in the community is capable of satisfying the state's compulsory attendance laws. Yet this is the very education which the trial court implicitly condemned when it convicted the defendants and which the public school authorities rejected in refusing a compromise settlement before the trial.

If no such private school compromise is in line with Amish religion, then the lines of conflict are basic. In its broadest terms, the contest is between the state's definition of education and the Amish definition of education; between the ultimate purposes of life as adhered to by the majority of a materialist society and the religious convictions held by the so-called Plain People; between the limitless and homogenizing logic of compulsory attendance and the rights of individuals and groups to maintain the sanctity of their own socially harmless values against a "pall of orthodoxy."

To view this contest as one between secular and clerical law is to misconceive the issue by using terms that have outlived their ability to describe reality. The fact that the value system of the Amish community is described by reference to the will of a Supreme Being raises its importance in the eyes of the law by invoking the protection of the Free Exercise Clause of the First Amendment. But the fact that the majority's choice of values is advanced by something called "compulsory school attendance" does not mean it has any less profound an influence on life goals and human beliefs. The issue is not new. More than 100 years ago John Stuart Mill observed:

> A general state education is a mere contrivance for molding people to be exactly like one another; and as the mold in which it casts them is that which pleases the predominant power in the government—whether this be a monarch, a priesthood, an aristocracy, or the majority of the existing generation—in proportion as it is efficient and successful, it establishes a despotism over the mind, leading by natural tendency to one over the body.

Of course, neither the U.S. Supreme Court nor the parties to the suit view the case in such broad terms. The decision will not concern the validity of compulsory attendance for all but only for the adolescent adherents of a small religious sect. To win the case, the state needed to go no further than to produce a strong justification for denying an exemption to the Amish.

The state's effort to present an interest compelling enough to warrant suppression of Amish religious practice is based upon the claim that an educational system is essential to the survival of this or any other society. In its attempt to shore up this precarious position, the state confronts the fact that compulsory education is supported more by inertia and assumption than by reason. Instead of confining itself to the threat posed by an exemption for the Amish, the state's brief leaps headlong into a general discussion of compulsory attendance. This effort succeeds only in raising the question of just why the state can compel school attendance for anyone, ever.

Three general reasons are advanced, in this case, by the Wisconsin State Attorney General's office, as justifications for compulsory attendance: preservation of the political system, economic survival, and socialization of children.

Of the three, the justification for compulsory school attendance rests most securely on the importance of preserving the political process embodied in a democratic form of government. In order for a system based on individual voting and private evaluation of public issues to operate, it is necessary that the vast majority of citizens be familiar with the system—be able to read and otherwise possess the minimum skills needed to acquire knowledge and make informed decisions. This argument about minimum skills has force, but the Amish case is a telling example of how it loses this force through indiscriminate application.

It is fair to assume that by the eighth grade reading and other basic skills, as well as familiarity with the democratic process, have been learned. Nothing to the contrary appears in the case. Yet the state relies upon this argument to compel school attendance by children in the ninth and tenth grades. One wants to ask how, specifically, two more years of schooling are going to advance Jefferson's notion, quoted in the state's brief, that "where the press is free and every man able to read, all is safe." If there is something which must be learned at this grade level to preserve democracy, by all means let it be required. But if not, the argument about preserving the political system is pushed to absurdity. It has no limits and so loses its credibility.

The second justification used by the state also relates to preserving the society, this time its economic rather than political well-being. Put in the most favorable light possible, the state claims that it is justified in requiring schooling so that young people will not become frustrated, unemployable adults and a burden on the society. This argument is embellished with references to higher income for high school graduates. In the case of the Amish, however, there is no burden upon society resulting from unemployed adults, nor is there an absence of training for useful work in the Amish community. As the able attorney for the Amish, William Ball, stated to the High Court, "The purpose of

Amish education is not to get ahead in the world but to get
to heaven."

In fact, the Amish have a long tradition of taking care of
their own dependents. Moreover, the Amish agricultural
community makes ample provision for training its adolescents
in farming and other skills and values necessary to the community's
survival. Those who leave the community may indeed be
temporarily at a loss. But if this is the state's concern, it might
simply provide free education and job training for those who
leave, rather than compel all Amish youth to endure high school
when it is admittedly useless and harmful to them. While we may
all applaud the effort to provide useful work skills to every
citizen and to avoid the burden on the state of high
unemployment, it is something else to suggest, as a 1967 *Virginia
Law Review* article on Amish education has, that "in sheer
economic terms, the nation's children are a natural resource
which the state may legitimately exploit to its full potential
by means of compulsory education." Such logic encourages the
state to substitute its vision, or perhaps that of corporate America,
for the religious views of the Amish about work and education
and personal contentment. Just such a vision was presented by
Wisconsin Assistant Attorney General John W. Calhoun when he
reprimanded the Amish for their insistence on a simple life,
and argued that "what is needed is more education to cope with
the problems of society—more pride in intellect, not less."

Running through the discussions of political and
economic reasons for compulsory education, and appearing in the
Yoder testimony, is the notion that the state has a compelling
interest in socializing children—in doing what it can to cast them
into a behavioral mold acceptable to the majority. The issue
of socialization is the most complex and troublesome one
in the case. The Amish challenge to our right to prescribe and
teach acceptable values ought to make us think twice about the
validity of the old notion that society can be improved by means
of schooling.

One could not deny that any institutional educational
setting carries in its structure, pedagogy, materials, and rules of
behavior the imprint of the value system that is adhered to by

those who control it. As education innovator Ivan Illich put it:
"All over the world schools are organized enterprises designed
to reproduce the established order, whether this order is called
revolutionary, conservative, or evolutionary." The Amish themselves
are no exception. The contest is simply between their values and
methods of child-rearing and those prescribed by the state.

Though the state nowhere explicitly claims that it has a
right to obliterate cultural differences, or to homogenize children,
or to replace the communal spirit with the competitive or
austerity with materialism, the testimony in the case suggests
just this purpose. In view of the inadequacy of the other reasons
put forward by the state, one wonders how else to explain its
vigorous prosecution of the Amish.

The present pattern of socialization through compulsory
schooling admits some diversity for those who are willing to
attend private school, can afford it, and will accept substantial
state regulation. For the Amish, however, this avenue for preserving
their social patterns does not exist. So the state's interest in
socializing could not be questioned more strongly than here.
For all its statements about freedom and democracy, the state of
Wisconsin is seeking to force the Amish to choose between
criminal sanctions on the one hand and abandoning their religious
practices and the view of education which sustain their community
on the other.

That socialization of children is basic to the state's attempt
to include the Amish in its captive audience raises the most
serious questions about the preservation of social pluralism.
If a state, whose policies are supposed to be an expression of
majority values, may regulate not only conduct that is inimical
to legitimate state interests but also a significant part of
personality formation, what source of support for diversity remains?
And if we may compel attendance from six to sixteen, why not
from one to thirty?

The state may forbid the exclusion of any group from a
public program; but as soon as it can compel the *inclusion* of
some group in a program whose inevitable effect is to mold
opinion and values, the entire basis of individual freedom has
been eroded. The Court has already ruled once that such logic

cannot justify compelling all children to attend public school;
now it must decide the issue of standardization anew.

The state's attempt at a general justification for compulsory
schooling does not find justifiable application in the *Yoder* case
and is too weak to support the burden of finding a compelling
interest. The protection of the political process might be made
specific enough to be credited, but as it stands it is neither
relevant to children above the eighth grade nor limited enough to
avoid becoming a justification for the perpetuation of ideology.
The economic and social rationales are similarly vague, overly
broad, and frightening in their potential for dissolving the basis
of individual rights.

The vagueness of these reasons becomes apparent when
they are compared with the compelling interests advanced by
states in other cases involving the conflict of religious tenets
and state law. A law requiring vaccination or X-rays, for example,
has been upheld over a claim that it violated religious scruples
against medical treatment, on the grounds that the state has a
compelling interest in preventing the spread of disease.

This case involved state regulation of specific acts as
justified by specific, limited, and compelling state interests.
This is to be contrasted with *Yoder*, in which attendance at an
institution with important influence over personality formation is
being justified by an open-ended desire to facilitate the orderly
continuation of the status quo.

The state advances an additional argument, however,
which appears to be more specific. It is here that it tries to
show why the Amish exemption threatens the system of
compulsory education and should not be granted. It claims that
since the child has a right to an education, and since Amish
community education does not prepare its young for any other
life than that of the Plain People, the purpose and effect of
compulsory schooling is to ensure the child an education which
will fit him for whatever life he chooses. The state claims in
its brief that "on failing to provide for secondary education
for their children, the Amish are neglecting a parental duty and
obligation to their children and their duty as citizens of a
democracy. . . ."

The corollary of this argument contends that compulsory attendance laws were enacted as an aid in enforcing child labor laws and are therefore part of a general scheme designed to prevent parents from yielding to economic pressure to send their children to work.

The right-to-education argument and the child labor argument are basically the same in that they both rely upon the notion that the state may regulate the family in order to protect the child from abuse or exploitation by the parents. In fact, when the Court upheld child labor laws against claims that they violated religious commandments to proselytize, the language of the Court made reference to compulsory attendance as another example of a compelling state interest in protecting children's safety and health.

This argument sets up a tension between the control of children by parents and by the state, confident that in this tension the child will find his maximum freedom and welfare. Here liberals probably stop and begin to scratch their heads. Even if one supposes that a basic equality between state and parent in the control of children might possibly promote the freedom of the children, that equality hardly exists today. At one point it was the duty solely of parents to educate the child. With the advent of modern state-regulated schooling, in which everything from dismissal for long hair to prescription of course work can be commanded by a pink slip from the principal's office, the pendulum has swung to the other extreme. What is needed is not to save the children from their parents but to save them from the deadening hand of the schools. As almost every article about education in the last five years has admitted, it is the schools, not the parents, that are damaging the children by excessively rigid control of their education.

One could sympathize with the idea that compulsory schooling should serve the purpose of providing every young person with the time and freedom and resources to explore and learn freely. According to this idea, the child is freed from work and family pressure and given some psychological space. But school is not value-free; and almost nowhere does it consist of freedom to explore. It is, rather, a maze of requirements and expectations and coercion. Though we might like "school" to mean freedom, in reality it makes a mockery of the "holy curiosity of inquiry" about which Einstein said: "It is a very grave mistake to think that the enjoyment of seeing and searching can be promoted by means of coercion and a sense of duty."

Perhaps the greatest irony of the case is the notion of freeing Amish children from their community. The Amish community experiences little delinquency in minors, causes and fights no wars, uses no polluting machines, eschews materialism, and has no economically based class system. To save these people from the quiet sanity of their lives by forcing them into the center of the psychologically unhealthy atmosphere of modern America strains the definition of freedom beyond recognition.

Even if a balance of state and parental influence over child-rearing were in fact established, such a formula would still be troublesome. A person's freedom—even a child's— cannot be secured by making him the object of a struggle for control. A sharp line must be drawn between giving the state power to punish specific, identifiable abuses of children by their parents, and elevating the state to a socializing role equal to that of the parents. The former has always been recognized as a justifiable exercise of the state's power to protect individuals from criminal acts by others. The latter runs against the entire notion of the family as the basic unit of society and the individual as the basic unit of democracy.

If such a wholesale restructuring of society and transference of the source of political power is to become law, it ought to be as the product of a revolution or a new constitution, not as an incidental rationalization for pushing a handful of farm children into the New Glarus, Wisconsin, public high school.

The existence of this paternalistic tug-of-war between the state and parents for the control of children exposes the fact that young people themselves have few rights and almost no legally acknowledged individuality. But more than this, it exposes the fact that our society has steadily weakened in its ability to understand and deal constructively with its children. Debate about state-versus-parent control unintentionally obscures the increasingly painful observation that neither of these claimants is really trusted to provide a supportive, humanistic, and self-actualizing child-rearing atmosphere, and that both may be becoming dysfunctional and alienating. One has only to talk to the "street kids" or the school kids to wonder whether there is any natural, comfortable place for children in America. Certainly it is not the standard public school.

The search for new forms of community going on in the counterculture is a partial recognition of this problem and an attempt to develop new child-rearing concepts and institutions. This important groping is nowhere near producing an organic solution. But the *Yoder* case is fast approaching the point of decision. It is clear, therefore, that the case must be decided on the basis of the obscuring dichotomy between parental and state control. There is no way to discuss the merits of some new child-rearing institution that might more justifiably be called "school." If there must be such a decision between these inadequate alternatives, state control is the more dangerous.

Compulsory schooling has been with us for so long that we rarely, if ever, examine why it exists, whether it should be altered, and how it is different from the increasingly important "Right to an Education." The reasons advanced by the state of Wisconsin to support this time-honored institution are so vague and so easily used to justify unconscionable restrictions on individual liberty and free exercise of religion that even in the narrow context of the *Yoder* case they are frightening.

By putting their own values on the line, the Amish have presented the public-at-large with a case which ought to prompt a much-needed reexamination of compulsory schooling. The fact that the case involves religious liberty on the one hand and state reproduction of established values on the other makes this reexamination hard to avoid. As Mr. Ball stated at the close of his argument to the Court: "If the Amish lose, [I fear that] people will feel the Court has indicted our nation as too ossified to permit honest differences."

9

The Many Meanings of the
Yoder Case

Leo Pfeffer

Leo Pfeffer is an attorney in New York City and a
professor of political science at Long Island University.
He is the author of *Church, State, and Freedom; The
Liberties of an American;* and *God, Caesar, and the
Constitution.*

In this essay he assesses the meaning of the Wisconsin
case in terms of the limits of the First Amendment free
exercise of religion clause and the implications of the
decision for American church-state relations.

Wisconsin v. *Yoder et al.* is a landmark case in American
Constitutional history. My purpose here is to look forward,
to see, not what questions the *Yoder* case resolved, but what
questions it poses. It is normal for constitutional landmark cases
to raise new and related questions which will come back in the
future to the court.

Perhaps the most common issue in the *Yoder* case is the
meaning of the First Amendment free exercise of religion clause.
What are the limitations of freedom of religion? How far does
freedom of religion go? How far is it protected? A secondary

question is the relationship of church and state. That question
will be discussed later.

The First Amendment has two guarantees: that Congress
shall make no law respecting the establishment of religion,
and the Congress may not prohibit the free exercise thereof.
It guarantees freedom from an established religion and it
guarantees freedom to exercise religion. Both are involved in
the *Yoder* case.

The case also raises questions independent of religion.
How far can a democratic state intervene in the private life
of a citizen for his or her own welfare? How far can the state
intervene to protect children when their welfare is thought to be
in danger because of some activity or nonactivity of the parents?
Finally, what are the implications of cultural pluralism versus
cultural uniformity?

Let us begin with the state's concern for the welfare of
its citizens. The Wisconsin law provides that all children up to
the age of sixteen must attend elementary and secondary school.
At the age of sixteen it deems them to be adults free to make
their own decisions about education.

At one time our common law considered twenty-one to
be the adult age. In the latest amendment to the Constitution
an eighteen-year-old is considered fully able to exercise the right
of a citizen in respect to the right to vote. At the age of eighteen
a male person can be compelled to serve in the armed forces.
With respect to education, the State of Wisconsin has said that
at sixteen a person is an adult, but there is nothing to prevent
Wisconsin or any other state from raising the age to eighteen
or even twenty. In the *Yoder* case, one of the children who
testified at the trial was fifteen years old. She testified that
because of her religious beliefs she did not want to go to high
school. In this case the Supreme Court decided that the young
girl was for all practical purposes an adult. The question then was,
aside from religious freedom, how far may a democratic state
act for the welfare of the citizens against their will?

Over a hundred years ago John Stuart Mill, in his classic
work, *On Liberty*, sought to give an answer to this question.
In a much quoted statement he said that the only purpose for

which power can be rightfully exercised over any member of
a civilized society against his will is to prevent harm to others.
His own good, either physical or moral, is not sufficient.
The state has no power in a civilized society to make a person
do something because it is for his own good. This is nineteenth-
century liberalism, popular then because it justified laissez-faire
economics, social Darwinism, and a hands-off attitude on the
part of the state.

In the United States, the Supreme Court, while not explicitly
saying so, adopted the same philosophy, particularly in the period
from the 1890s to the 1930s. In a number of decisions, the
Court threw out laws seeking to limit the number of hours a
person could work. The courts said that if a grown man wanted
to work twelve hours a day for six days a week, it was his
business. The state could not hinder him even though it might
be hazardous to his health. Ironically, the only point at which
the state could prevent a person from working was on Sunday.
In the same way, if a man sought to work for wages below the
subsistence level the state could not intervene.

There were, of course, cases in which this philosophy was
challenged. In a 1905 case, *Jacobson* v. *Massachusetts*, a state law
requiring innoculation was challenged. Jacobson refused inn
innoculation, not for religious reasons, but because, he argued,
the innoculation was dangerous and he did not need it. The state
prosecuted him for violating the law. The Supreme Court upheld
the state law.

In another case the Supreme Court refused to hear an
appeal from a lower court ruling that in an emergency doctors
may give a patient a blood transfusion against his will if his life
is in danger. But what if religious considerations were a factor
in such a case? In 1964 a member of the Jehovah's Witnesses
refused a blood transfusion on religious grounds, despite the
physician's prognosis that the woman could not survive without
a transfusion. The hospital acquired a court order granting
permission to give the blood transfusion against the woman's
will. The case was then appealed to the New Jersey Supreme Court
which upheld the court order. But on what basis? Surely in this
case it was clear that failure to have a blood transfusion

would not harm anyone else, the criterion of both John Stuart Mill and the United States Supreme Court for action by the state on the will of an individual. How then did the New Jersey Supreme Court justify state intervention? It so happened the woman was pregnant, and that the court argued that failure to take the blood transfusion would condemn the fetus to death. Since the fetus, according to the court, was an unborn human being, and its survival was involved, the state, again using Mill's dictum, could force the woman to accept a blood transfusion.

The case, however, skirted the main question we are concerned with: Can a democratic society compel a person to take action for his own good? For example, in the *Yoder* case, assuming the Amish children are adults, is it permissible for the State of Wisconsin to insist that in order for them to survive in American society, they must have a high school education? Can they, for their own good, be compelled to attend high school? This is a question inherent in all our compulsory education laws, in addition to, and perhaps even prior to, the question of parental control of a child's education.

To take a hypothetical case, suppose a child inherits great wealth and will never need to earn a living. Can the state compel such a child to be educated? The question also arises when a person who has no children is taxed to support a school system. When the first free public education systems were established in the nineteenth century, many legislators objected to paying taxes to educate other people's children. In a debate over the issue in the Pennsylvania legislature, Thaddeus Stevens, the abolitionist, delivered what has become the classic justification for universal free education. Basing his remarks on ideas derived from Thomas Jefferson, Stevens argued that the entire community benefits from an educated citizenry, so all should help assume its costs.

This rationale, incidentally, serves as a strong counter argument to those who believe that public funds should be used to finance nonpublic education. The position often stated is that if parents must pay for parochial education in addition to paying public school taxes, they are being doubly taxed. The answer Stevens gave is that whether or not you have children in

public school, or children at all, an educated citizenry is of
benefit to the entire society.

The Supreme Court recognized this in the *Yoder* case,
using the Jeffersonian philosophy as its rationale. They also pointed
out that another reason public schools were established was to take
children off the labor market. The Court observed that labor
unions were among the strongest advocates of universal compulsory
education because they realized that child labor depressed wages.
On these grounds, society had an interest in compelling the
Amish children to attend school rather than work on a farm.

There are other areas where the courts have also, in effect,
superseded the John Stuart Mill philosophy. An example is
Social Security, where the state forces the individual to save for
old age by withholding taxes during the productive years.
The same is true for Medicare, minimum wage, and maximum
hour laws. In all these cases the state compels the individual
to act for his own benefit.

We turn now to the state's concern for the welfare of
children. Justice Douglas, in his dissenting opinion in the *Yoder*
case, raised the question of what the Supreme Court might have
said had the Amish children indicated their desire to continue
in school despite their parents' wishes. Can the state supersede
the wishes of the parents for the good of the child?

Rooted in common law is the notion of *parens patriae*,
giving the state the power to set aside the wishes of the parents
for the welfare of the child. Numerous cases have been upheld
by the courts on this basis, notably in the case of Jehovah's
Witnesses who sought to resist having their children given blood
transfusions. But just how far the state can go on this matter
is unclear. What is clear is that the state has the power to enforce
compulsory elementary education despite the wishes of the parents.
As Justice Douglas intimated, it is conceivable that the Court will
be faced with a case in which a fifteen-year-old Amish child
will desire to continue his or her education against the wishes
of the parents. What the Court will say to that remains to be
seen, for in the *Yoder* case it said it would deal with the
problem when it arose.

Take a hypothetical case. Suppose a child is ill and the physicians advise a certain treatment repugnant to the parents on the basis of their religion. Withholding treatment will not cost the child's life; it will merely cause him to suffer, perhaps even disable him. Can the state intervene on behalf of the child? A practical case in point is the case of fluoridated water. Dental research has proven that fluoridated water helps prevent cavities. Some Christian Scientists believe drinking fluoridated water is sinful. Can the state defy the wishes of the parents and require the children to drink fluoridated water? In this case the child won't die; he won't even get sick. He probably will have to visit his dentist more frequently than his fluoridated water-drinking peers. Again the question is where should the line of state intervention be drawn.

In the *Yoder* case the Supreme Court pointed out that the Amish style of dress subjects Amish children to ridicule by their secular peers. Is this sufficient cause for the state to force the Amish to dress their children in more conventional attire?

An analogous case came before the Supreme Court in 1948 in *McCollum* v. *Board of Education.* Champaign, Illinois, had a program of released time for religious instruction. The classes were held in the regular classroom and those who did not want to participate were sent to an adjoining room during that period. Terry McCollum was a ten-year-old boy whose mother was an atheist and would not allow Terry to participate in the religious instruction. Terry, however, wanted to participate, not because he desired religious instruction, but because he was constantly reviled by his classmates as an atheist becuase of his nonparticipation. Could the Court under those circumstances declare, as Mrs. McCollum sought, that religious instruction in public schools is unconstitutional?

Similar factors were involved in *West Virginia* v. *Barnette,* the flag salute case. There, Jehovah's Witness parents would not allow their children to salute the flag. As a result the children were reviled and persecuted as un-American and unpatriotic. Should the state have ruled that the children must salute the flag despite their parents' wishes in order to save the children the discomfort of public ridicule? How far can the state go on this kind of issue?

The courts are quite clear that on matters of life and death the state may intercede on behalf of the child. But now the courts have gone beyond that, in effect saying that while the child can be compelled to attend elementary school, he cannot be compelled to attend secondary school if by so doing he violates the religious scruples of the parents.

A third problem posed by the *Yoder* decision is the matter of cultural pluralism versus cultural uniformity. The Supreme Court pointed out clearly that what was involved was not individual practice but a lifestyle which is integral to an entire community, drawn from the experience and resources of a centuries-old tradition. It seems clear that the state has an interest in cultural uniformity. Our coins proclaim "*e pluribus unum*" ("out of many one"). America is the great melting pot, we are told, where people from every corner of the globe are transformed into hard-working, clean-cut Americans. This was a particularly popular notion during the 1920s, when even the teaching and speaking of foreign languages was frowned upon.

Today the tide has turned, and the mood now is highly favorable to cultural pluralism. The question remains, nevertheless, whether the state has the right to determine what the preferred cultural model should be. How far is cultural pluralism protected by the Constitution? This was one of the key questions raised by the *Yoder* case.

We turn now to the matter of free exercise of religion. The First Amendment has several guarantees. Congress shall make no law respecting the establishment of religion, nor prohibit the free exercise thereof, nor abridge freedom of speech or press, nor restrict the right of the people to assemble peaceably. Citizens shall be free to petition the government for redress of grievances. All of these rights are protected by the First Amendment.

During the 1920s and '30s the Supreme Court established what was called the "preferred position" of the First Amendment rights. This meant that "First Amendment rights are fundamental and courts ought to make particular efforts to protect them.

This is still in effect today. One reason cases dealing with obscenity and pornography are dealt with so gingerly is that freedom of speech and press are "preferred" rights.

But are any of the six rights more important than the others? For many years the Supreme Court held that all rights within the First Amendment were equal. For example, in *Prince* v. *Massachusetts* in 1944, a Jehovah's Witness allowed her niece to sell magazines and literature of the religious group on the street. She was arrested for violating the child labor law which said that no one under sixteen could sell magazines or newspapers on a public street. The woman's defense argued that the law interfered with the exercise of her religion. The defense acknowledged that in a previous test case the Supreme Court had rejected the claim that the law interfered with freedom of press, but they argued that freedom of religion was a higher value. The Court rejected the idea, saying that all the First Amendment rights were equal.

This was also upheld in the *Snyder* v. *New Jersey* case, where another Jehovah's Witness appealed a statute prohibiting the distribution of literature on the streets of Irving, New Jersey. The Supreme Court upheld the Jehovah's Witnesses' right to distribute their literature, not on freedom of religion, but on freedom of the press, grounds. The same rationale was applied in later cases.

It seems that on this issue the courts were not consistent with the American consensus. History shows that the American people have always considered freedom of religion superior to the other First Amendment freedoms. Freedom of religion has never been interfered with legislatively in American history. The government has never sought to determine what is heretical or orthodox. Yet government has interfered with speech and press, in laws against sedition and pornography. Another example of the bias toward freedom of religion is the case of conscientious objection to war. Since 1917 Congress has exempted those who are conscientiously opposed to war only on religious grounds. The law states specifically that the opposition to war must be a result of religious training and belief and not politically, sociologically, or philosophically motivated. This reflects the

American consensus that religious freedom is the most important and precious of all the freedoms.

Since 1963 the Supreme Court has moved closer to the American consensus that freedom of religion is a specially "preferred" right. In the *Sherbert* v. *Verner* case the Court ruled that the State of South Carolina could not constitutionally deny unemployment benefits to a Seventh Day Adventist who refused to take a job requiring her to work on Saturday. By compelling the woman to take work which violated her religious convictions, the Court said the state was violating the woman's free exercise of religion. Now it is quite clear that had she argued that she rejected the job because it was unaesthetic, or violated her philosophical beliefs, the Court would not have upheld her plea. It was her religious convictions which the Court was defending. Clearly the Court was elevating religion above the other rights. Whereas earlier the Court was at best neutral, it has now come out on the side of religion.

One can cite other illustrations of the same trend. In 1963 the Supreme Court reversed a lower court decision which had found a person in contempt of court for refusing jury duty on religious grounds. Again had the plea been based on any other basis the Court would surely have upheld the lower court decision. In the *Gillette* case the Court declared that the only legal basis for conscientious objection was religious. It declared that whether a war was moral or immoral was not a religious but a political question. It becomes a religious question at the point where all war is declared immoral, a position held by the historic peace churches.

The *Yoder* case marks the capstone of this new move toward giving religious freedom a higher value than other First Amendment rights. It is quite clear from the language of the Supreme Court decision that had the Amish objected to sending their children to high school for any reason other than the religious one, they would not have succeeded in their case. The critical factor, and the Court made a special effort to be explicit about this, was that the Amish way of life and their faith were inseparable and interdependent. A way of life, the Court asserted, however virtuous and admirable, may not be interposed as a barrier to a state law if it is based upon secular considerations. The Court cited Henry Thoreau as an example. Despite the unity of Thoreau's lifestyle and philosophy, the state had a right to force him to conform, in his case to pay his taxes. The Amish, in effect, took the same position as Thoreau, but because their rationale was religious rather than philosophical, their position was protected.

The decision explicitly elevates religious freedom above the other freedoms, declaring that the courts must give special consideration to those who for religious reasons find themselves in conflict with the laws of the land.

The *Yoder* case touches separation of church and state as well as religious freedom. The Supreme Court recognized that. The Court indicated that not only was the free exercise of religion a superior right, but the establishment clause was equally important. "Long before there was general acknowledgment of the need for universal formal education," the Court declared, "the religion clauses had specifically and firmly fixed the right to free exercise of religious beliefs, and buttressing this fundamental right was an equally firm, even if less explicit, prohibition against the establishment of any religion by government. The values underlying these two provisions relating to religion have been zealously protected, sometimes even at the expense of other interests of admittedly high social importance."

In this passage the Court indicated that it considered the establishment clause of equal importance with the free exercise clause. The Court invalidated state government subsidies to parochial schools even though it recognized the undoubted public interest in sound education for children attending parochial schools. The Court's rationale lay in the argument that though good education is important, of greater importance is the principle of separation of church and state. Just as the Court has protected free exercise of religion against the secular value that everyone should have a high school eduation in the *Yoder* case, in several other cases the Court has protected the establishment clause against the same claim of a good education. In short, as of now the Supreme Court has decreed that both religious clauses of the First Amendment—the free exercise and the no establishment of religion clauses—are of equal value. Each reinforces the other. Each is superior to all other rights and freedoms.

The Supreme Court recognized that there can be and is tension between the free exercise of religion and the nonestablishment clause. In 1947 the Court defined establishment of religion. The government, the Court declared, may not aid religion; it must be strictly neutral, not merely among religions, but also between religion and nonreligion. One of the arguments of the State of Wisconsin in the *Yoder* case was that by exempting the Amish from the compulsory education law, the courts were aiding religion. They were not being neutral.

In the *Yoder* case the Court stated that the Amish children do not need to go to school beyond fourteen years of age. Suppose their non-Amish neighbors decided to keep their children at home beyond the age of fourteen? The Court's response was quite clear; only if the motivations are clearly religious can the law be waived. Isn't that preferring religion over nonreligion? Is that neutrality?

Or take the *Sherbert* case. Here the Supreme Court said quite clearly that if Mrs. Sherbert were to refuse work for reasons other than religion, she could be denied unemployment benefits by the state. Isn't that aiding religion? Or the *Gillette* case, which rejected the right of conscientious objection to those who opposed only immoral wars, not all wars, as religious objectors do. Wasn't that giving religion preferential treatment? The same question was raised in the *Welsh* case. The Supreme Court upheld the statute exempting from taxes property owned by churches and used for religious purposes. The argument was made that such a law constituted aid to religion and therefore was a violation of the establishment clause. In the *Genesis* case a lady refused to serve on the jury. If she refused on religious grounds, she was free not to serve. If she used any other reason, she would not be excused. Wasn't that giving religion preeminence?

The tension between free exercise and no establishment becomes most clear in the issue of aid to parochial schools. Most arguments in favor of aid to parochial schools have long been based upon the *Pierce* case. In 1925 the Supreme Court

ruled that parents have a constitutional right to send their children
to parochial schools and any law which forbids sending children
to parochial schools is unconstitutional. It violates the free
exercise of religion of the parents. Proponents of aid to parochial
schools argue that if parents are too poor to pay for the parochial
school tuition and the state refuses assistance, it is violating the
free exercise of religion of these parents. On the other hand,
the opponents argue that if the state does give money to send
children to parochial schools, the state is violating the establishment
clause. How can the dilemma be reconciled?

Reconciliation of the establishment clause and the free
exercise clause is suggested in a statement by Thomas Paine,
the Revolutionary War pamphleteer, whose *Common Sense* became
one of the great patriotic documents of the war. Paine said:
"After religion, I hold it to be the indispensible duty of the
government to protect all conscientious professors there are,
and I know of no other business which government has to do
therewith." When Paine speaks of protecting "all conscientious
professors," he means the free exercise of religion. The phrase
"I know of no other business which government has to do
therewith" means that government must keep out of religion in
every respect.

In the *Yoder* case and the other cases surveyed here,
the courts seem to be saying that the free exercise of religion is,
with rare exceptions, the right to be left alone. When the state
does not tax religious property, the Supreme Court argued in
the *Welsh* case, it is buttressing the free exercise of religion.
It is letting religion alone. When the Court told the State of
Wisconsin that it could not force the Amish to send their children
to high school in violation of their religion, the state was being
enjoined to leave the Amish undisturbed. When Mrs. Genesis
refused to serve on a jury because of her religious convictions,
the Court enjoined the state to leave her alone. In this sense
the state was not aiding religion, but merely letting it alone.
However, when the state does not let religion alone, but uses its
power to support religion, as when it takes funds from the
government treasury and puts them into a religious school in order

to give children a religious education, it is going beyond the
free exercise clause and violating the establishment clause.

The *Pierce* case stated that if we want our children to attend
parochial schools, religious freedom entitled them to do so,
and the state cannot compel us to send them to public school.
In the *Yoder* case the Supreme Court asserted that the state
cannot force us to send our children to school beyond the age
of fourteen if the reason is religious. In short, what the free
exercise of religion basically protects is the right to be left alone,
and as long as the state acts in such a way that lets people alone,
it is not violating the establishment clause. When the state goes
beyond that, when it uses public resources to assist people in
carrying out their religious practice, it is going beyond free
exercise and violating the establishment clause, becuase it is going
beyond being left alone.

In summary, the *Yoder* case has implications for the present
in three areas. First, it elevates the religion clauses, free exercise
and establishment of religion, above the other rights guaranteed
in the First Amendment. Second, these two clauses are now
perceived as equal in value. Third, when there is an apparent
conflict between the free exercise and the establishment clause,
the line of demarcation is whether the state extends its control
beyond letting people alone to exercise their religion. When it
doesn't go beyond that, it is within the free exercise clause;
if it goes beyond and affirmatively aids a religious group,
it violates the establishment clause. These are the implications of
the *Yoder* case and this is why it is truly a landmark in the
history of American religion and American religious freedom.

Appendix

State of Wisconsin, Petitioner, v *Jonas Yoder et al.:*

Text of the Supreme Court Decision

After the Wisconsin Supreme Court found in favor of
the Amish, the State of Wisconsin appealed the decision to
the U.S. Supreme Court. The case was argued before the
Court on December 8, 1971, and the decision handed down
on May 15, 1972. The U.S. Supreme Court upheld the
decision of the Wisconsin Supreme Court.

SUMMARY

The defendants, who were members of the Amish faith,
refused to send their children, aged 14 and 15, to public school
after the children had completed the eighth grade. In Green County
Court, Wisconsin, the defendants were convicted for violating
Wisconsin's compulsory school attendance law requiring children
to attend school until the age of 16. The Wisconsin Circuit Court
affirmed the convictions, but the Wisconsin Supreme Court,
sustaining the defendants' claims that their First Amendment right
to free exercise of religion had been violated, reversed the
convictions (49 Wis 2d 430, 182 NW2d 539).
On certiorari, the United States Supreme Court affirmed.

In an opinion by BURGER, Ch. J., expressing the views of six
members of the court, it was held (1) that secondary schooling,
by exposing Amish children to worldly influences in terms of
attitudes, goals, and values contrary to sincere religious beliefs,
and by substantially interfering with the religious development of
the Amish child and his integration into the way of life of the
Amish faith community at the crucial adolescent state of
development, contravened the basic religious tenets and practice
of the Amish faith, both as to the parent and the child;
(2) that since accommodating the religious objections of the Amish
by forgoing one, or at most two, additional years of compulsory
education would not impair the physical or mental health of the
child, nor result in an inability to be self-supporting, or to
discharge the duties and responsibilities of citizenship, or in any
other way materially detract from the welfare of society, the
state's interest in its system of compulsory education was not so
compelling that the established religious practices of the Amish
had to give way; and (3) that since it was the parents who were
subject to prosecution for failing to cause their children to attend
school, and since the record did not indicate that the parents'
preventing their children from attending school was against the
children's expressed desires, it was the parents' right of the
exercise of religion, not the children's right, which had to
determine Wisconsin's power to impose criminal penalties on the
parent.

STEWART, J., joined by BRENNAN, J., concurring, joined
in the court's opinion and stated that the case in no way involved
any questions regarding the right of the children of Amish parents
to attend public high schools, or any other institutions of learning,
if they wished to do so.

WHITE, J., joined by BRENNAN and STEWART, JJ.,
concurring, joined in the court's opinion on the grounds that it
could not be said that the state's interest in requiring 2 more
years of compulsory education in the ninth and tenth grades
outweighed the importance of the concededly sincere Amish
religious practice to the survival of that sect.

DOUGLAS, J., dissenting in part, stated that the religious
views of the child whose parent was the subject of the suit were

crucial, and that although the judgment below was properly affirmed as to one of the defendants, whose child had testified that her own religious views were opposed to high-school education, the case should be remanded as to the other defendants, so that their children could be given an opportunity to be heard.

POWELL and REHNQUIST, JJ., did not participate.

APPEARANCES OF COUNSEL

John William Calhoun argued the cause for the petitioner. William B. Ball argued the cause for the respondent.

OPINION OF THE COURT

Mr. Chief Justice Burger delivered the opinion of the Court.

On petition of the State of Wisconsin, we granted the writ in this case to review a decision of the Wisconsin Supreme Court holding that respondents' convictions for violating the State's compulsory school attendance law were invalid under the Free Exercise Clause of the First Amendment to the United States Constitution made applicable to the State by the Fourteenth Amendment. For the reasons hereafter stated we affirm the judgment of the Supreme Court of Wisconsin.

Respondents Jonas Yoder and Adin Yutzy are members of the Old Order Amish Religion, and respondent Wallace Miller is a member of the Conservative Amish Mennonite Church. They and their families are residents of Green County, Wisconsin. Wisconsin's compulsory school attendance law required them to cause their children to attend public or private school until reaching age 16 but the respondents declined to send their children, ages 14 and 15, to public school after completing the eighth grade. The children were not enrolled in any private school, or within any recognized exception to the compulsory attendance law, and they are conceded to be subject to the Wisconsin statute.

On complaint of the school district administrator for the public schools, respondents were charged, tried and convicted of violating the compulsory attendance law in Green County Court and were fined the sum of $5 each. Respondents defended on the ground that the application of the compulsory attendance law violated their rights under the First and Fourteenth Amendments. The trial testimony showed that respondents believed, in accordance with the tenets of Old Order Amish communities generally, that their children's attendance at high school, public or private, was contrary to the Amish religion and way of life. They believed that by sending their children to high school, they would not only expose themselves to the danger of the censure of the church community, but, as found by the county court, endanger their own salvation and that of their children. The State stipulated that respondents' religious beliefs were sincere.

In support of their position, respondents presented as expert witnesses scholars on religion and education whose testimony is uncontradicted. They expressed their opinions on the relationship of the Amish belief concerning school attendance to the more general tenets of their religion, and described the impact that compulsory high school attendance could have on the continued survival of Amish communities as they exist in the United States today. The history of the Amish sect was given in some detail, beginning with the Swiss Anabaptists of the 16th century who rejected institutionalized churches and sought to return to the early, simple, Christian life de-emphasizing material success, rejecting the competitive spirit, and seeking to insulate themselves from the modern world. As a result of their common heritage, Old Order Amish communities today are characterized by a fundamental belief that salvation requires life in a church community separate and apart from the world and worldly influence. This concept of life aloof from the world and its values is central to their faith.

A related feature of Old Order Amish communities is their devotion to a life in harmony with nature and the soil, as exemplified by the simple life of the early Christian era which continued in America during much of our early national life. Amish beliefs require members of the community to make their living by farming or closely related activities. Broadly speaking, the Old Order Amish religion pervades and determines the entire mode of life of its adherents. Their conduct is regulated in great detail by the Ordnung, or rules, of the church community. Adult baptism, which occurs in late adolescence, is the time at which Amish young people voluntarily undertake heavy obligations, not unlike the Bar Mitzvah of the Jews, to abide by the rules of the church community.

Amish objection to formal education beyond the eighth grade is firmly grounded in these central religious concepts. They object to the high school and higher education generally because the values it teaches are in marked variance with Amish values and the Amish way of life; they view secondary school education as an impermissible exposure of their children to a "worldly" influence in conflict with their beliefs. The high school tends to emphasize intellectual and scientific accomplishments, self-distinction, competitiveness, worldly success, and social life with other students. Amish society emphasizes informal learning-through-doing, a life of "goodness," rather than a life of intellect; wisdom, rather than technical knowledge; community welfare, rather than competition; and separation, rather than integration with contemporary worldly society.

Formal high school education beyond the eighth grade is contrary to Amish beliefs not only because it places Amish children in an environment hostile to Amish beliefs with increasing emphasis on competition in class work and sports and with pressure to conform to the styles, manners and ways of the peer group, but because it takes them away from their community, physically and emotionally, during the crucial and formative adolescent period of life. During this period, the children must acquire Amish attitudes favoring manual work and self-reliance and the specific skills needed to perform the adult role of an Amish farmer or housewife. They must learn to enjoy physical labor. Once a child has learned basic reading, writing, and elementary mathematics, these traits, skills, and attitudes admittedly fall within the category of those best learned through example and "doing" rather than in a classroom. And, at this time in life, the Amish child must also grow in his faith and his relationship to the Amish community if he is to be prepared to accept the heavy obligations imposed by adult baptism. In short, high school attendance with teachers who are not of the Amish

faith—and may even be hostile to it—interposes a serious barrier
to the integration of the Amish child into the Amish religious
community. Dr. John Hostetler, one of the experts on Amish
society, testified that the modern high school is not equipped,
in curriculum or social environment, to impart the values
promoted by Amish society.

The Amish do not object to elementary education through
the first eight grades as a general proposition because they agree
that their children must have basic skills in the "three R's"
in order to read the Bible, to be good farmers and citizens and
to be able to deal with non-Amish people when necessary in the
course of daily affairs. They view such a basic education as
acceptable because it does not significantly expose their children
to worldly values or interfere with their development in the
Amish community during the crucial adolescent period. While
Amish accept compulsory elementary education generally,
wherever possible they have established their own elementary
schools in many respects like the small local schools of the past.
In the Amish belief higher learning tends to develop values they
reject as influences that alienate man from God.

On the basis of such considerations, Dr. Hostetler testified
that compulsory high school attendance could not only result
in great psychological harm to Amish children, because of the
conflicts it would produce, but would, in his opinion, ultimately
result in the destruction of the Old Order Amish church
community as it exists in the United States today. The testimony
of Dr. Donald A. Erickson, an expert witness on education,
also showed that the Amish succeed in preparing their high school
age children to be productive members of the Amish community.
He described their system of learning-through-doing the skills
directly relevant to their adult roles in the Amish community
as "ideal" and perhaps superior to ordinary high school education.
The evidence also showed that the Amish have an excellent
record as law-abiding and generally self-sufficient members of
society.

Although the trial court in its careful findings determined
that the Wisconsin compulsory school attendance law "does
interfere with the freedom of the defendants to act in accordance

with their sincere religious belief" it also concluded that the requirement of high school attendance until age 16 was a "reasonable and constitutional" exercise of governmental power, and therefore denied the motion to dismiss the charges. The Wisconsin Circuit Court affirmed the convictions. The Wisconsin Supreme Court, however, sustained respondents' claim under the Free Exercise Clause of the First Amendment and reversed the convictions. A majority of the court was of the opinion that the State had failed to make an adequate showing that its interest in "establishing and maintaining an education system overrides the defendants' right to the free exercise of their religion."

I

There is no doubt as to the power of a State, having a high responsibility for education of its citizens, to impose reasonable regulations for the control and duration of basic education. See, e.g., *Pierce v Society of Sisters*, 268 US 510, 534, 69 L Ed 1070, 1077, 45 S Ct 571, 39 ALR 468 (1925). Providing public schools ranks at the very apex of the function of a State. Yet even this paramount responsbility was, in *Pierce*, made to yield to the right of parents to provide an equivalent education in a privately operated system. There the Court held that Oregon's statute compelling attendance in a public school from age eight to age 16 unreasonably interfered with the interest of parents in directing the rearing of their offspring including their education in church-operated schools. As that case suggests, the values of parental direction of the religious upbringing and education of their children in their early and formative years have a high place in our society. See also *Ginsberg v New York*, 390 US 629, 639, 20 L Ed 2d 195, 203, 88 S Ct 1274 (1968); *Meyer v Nebraska*, 262 US 390, 67 L Ed 1042, 43 S Ct 625, 29 ALR 1446 (1923); cf. *Rowan v Post Office Dept.*, 397 US 728, 25 L Ed 2d 736, 90 S Ct 1484 (1970). Thus, a State's interest in universal education, however highly we rank it, is not totally free from a balancing process when it impinges on other fundamental rights and interests, such as those specifically protected by the Free

Exercise Clause of the First Amendment and the traditional
interest of parents with respect to the religious upbringing
of their children so long as they, in the words of Pierce,
"prepare [them] for additional obligations." 268 US, at 535,
69 L Ed at 1078.

It follows that in order for Wisconsin to compel school
attendance beyond the eighth grade against a claim that such
attendance interferes with the practice of a legitimate religious
belief, it must appear either that the State does not deny the
free exercise of religious belief by its requirement, or that
there is a state interest of sufficient magnitude to override the
interest claiming protection under the Free Exercise Clause.
Long before there was general acknowledgment of the need
for universal formal education, the Religion Clauses had specifically
and firmly fixed the right to free exercise of religious beliefs,
and buttressing this fundamental right was an equally firm,
even if less explicit, prohibition against the establishment of
any religion by government. The values underlying these two
provisions relating to religion have been zealously protected,
sometimes even at the expense of other interests of admittedly
high social importance. The invalidation of financial aid to
parochial schools by government grants for a salary subsidy
for teachers is but one example of the extent to which courts
have gone in this regard, notwithstanding that such aid programs
were legislatively determined to be in the public interest and
the service of sound educational policy by States and by Congress.
Lemon v *Kurtzman*, 403 US 602, 29 L Ed 2d 745, 91 S Ct
2105 (1971); *Tilton* v *Richardson*, 403 US 672, 29 L Ed 2d 790,
91 S Ct 2091 (1971). See also *Everson* v *Board of Education*,
330 US 1, 18, 91 L Ed 711, 724, 67 S Ct 504, 168 ALR 1392
(1947).

The essence of all that has been said and written on the
subject is that only those interests of the highest order and those
not otherwise served can overbalance legitimate claims to the
free exercise of religion. We can accept it as settled, therefore,
that however strong the State's interest in universal compulsory
education, it is by no means absolute to the exclusion or
subordination of all other interests. E.g., *Sherbert* v *Verner*,

374 US 398, 10 L Ed 2d 965, 83 S Ct 1790 (1963); *McGowan v Maryland*, 366 US 420, 459, 6 L Ed 2d 393, 418, 81 S Ct 1101 (1961) (Frankfurter, J., concurring); *Prince v Massachusetts*, 321 US 158, 165, 88 L Ed 645, 651, 64 S Ct 438 (1944).

II

We come then to the quality of the claims of the respondents concerning the alleged encroachment of Wisconsin's compulsory school attendance statute on their rights and the rights of their children to the free exercise of the religious beliefs they and their forebears have adhered to for almost three centuries. In evaluating those claims we must be careful to determine whether the Amish religious faith and their mode of life are, as they claim, inseparable and interdependent. A way of life, however virtuous and admirable, may not be interposed as a barrier to reasonable state regulation of education if it is based on purely secular considerations; to have the protection of the Religion Clauses, the claims must be rooted in religious belief. Although a determination of what is a "religious" belief or practice entitled to constitutional protection may present a most delicate question, the very concept of ordered liberty precludes allowing every person to make his own standards on matters of conduct in which society as a whole has important interests. Thus, if the Amish asserted their claims because of their subjective evaluation and rejection of the contemporary secular values accepted by the majority, much as Thoreau rejected the social values of his time and isolated himself at Walden Pond, their claim would not rest on a religious basis. Thoreau's choice was philosophical and personal rather than religious, and such belief does not rise to the demands of the Religion Clause.

Giving no weight to such secular considerations, however, we see that the record in this case abundantly supports the claim that the traditional way of life of the Amish is not merely a matter of personal preference, but one of deep religious conviction, shared by an organized group, and intimately related to daily living. That the Old Order Amish daily life and religious practice stems from their faith is shown by the fact that it is in response to their literal interpretation of the Biblical injunction from the

Epistle of Paul to the Romans, "Be not conformed to this
world. . . ." This command is fundamental to the Amish faith.
Moreover, for the Old Order Amish, religion is not simply a
matter of theocratic belief. As the expert witnesses explained,
the Old Order Amish religion pervades and determines virtually
their entire way of life, regulating it with the detail of the
Talmudic diet through the strictly enforced rules of the church
community.

The record shows that the respondents' religious beliefs
and attitude toward life, family, and home have remained constant
—perhaps some would say static—in a period of unparalleled
progress in human knowledge generally and great changes in
education. The respondents freely concede, and indeed assert
as an article of faith, that their religious beliefs and what we
would today call "life style" has not altered in fundamentals
for centuries. Their way of life in a church-oriented community,
separated from the outside world and "worldly" influences,
their attachment to nature and the soil, is a way inherently
simple and uncomplicated, albeit difficult to preserve against the
pressure to conform. Their rejection of telephones, automobiles,
radios, and television, their mode of dress, of speech, their
habits of manual work do indeed set them apart from much of
contemporary society; these customs are both symbolic and
practical.

As the society around the Amish has become more populous,
urban, industrialized, and complex, particularly in this century,
government regulation of human affairs has correspondingly become
more detailed and pervasive. The Amish mode of life has thus
come into conflict increasingly with requirements of contemporary
society exerting a hydraulic insistence on conformity to
majoritarian standards. So long as compulsory education laws
were confined to eight grades of elementary basic education
imparted in a nearby rural schoolhouse, with a large proportion
of students of the Amish faith, the Old Order Amish had little
basis to fear that school attendance would expose their children
to the worldly influence they reject. But modern compulsory
secondary education in rural areas is now largely carried on in a
consolidated school, often remote from the student's home and

alien to his daily home life. As the record so strongly shows,
the values and programs of the modern secondary school are
in sharp conflict with the fundamental mode of life mandated by
the Amish religion; modern laws requiring compulsory secondary
education have accordingly engendered great concern and conflict.
The conclusion is inescapable that secondary schooling, by exposing
Amish children to worldly influences in terms of attitudes, goals
and values contrary to beliefs, and by substantially interfering
with the religious development of the Amish child and his
integration into the way of life of the Amish faith community
at the crucial adolescent state of development, contravenes the
basic religious tenets and practice of the Amish faith, both as
to the parent and the child.

The impact of the compulsory attendance law on respondents'
practice of the Amish religion is not only severe, but inescapable,
for the Wisconsin law affirmatively compels them, under threat
of criminal sanction, to perform acts undeniably at odds with
fundamental tenets of their religious beliefs. See *Braunfeld* v
Brown, 366 US 599, 605, 6 L Ed 2d 563, 567, 81 S Ct 1144
(1961). Nor is the impact of the compulsory attendance law
confined to grave interference with important Amish religious
tenets from a subjective point of view. It carries with it precisely
the kind of objective danger to the free exercise of religion
which the First Amendment was designed to prevent. As the
record shows, compulsory school attendance to age 16 for Amish
children carries with it a very real threat of undermining the
Amish community and religious practice as it exists today;
they must either abandon belief and be assimilated into society
at large, or be forced to migrate to some other and more tolerant
region.

In sum, the unchallenged testimony of acknowledged experts
in education and religious history, almost 300 years of consistent
practice, and strong evidence of a sustained faith pervading and
regulating respondents' entire mode of life support the claim
that enforcement of the State's requirement of compulsory formal
education after the eighth grade would gravely endanger if not
destroy the free exercise of respondents' religious beliefs.

III

Neither the findings of the trial court nor the Amish claims as to the nature of their faith are challenged in this Court by the State of Wisconsin. Its position is that the State's interest in universal compulsory formal secondary education to age 16 is so great that it is paramount to the undisputed claims of respondents that their mode of preparing their youth for Amish life, after the traditional elementary education, is an essential part of their religious belief and practice. Nor does the State undertake to meet the claim that the Amish mode of life and education is inseparable from and a part of the basic tenets of their religion—indeed, as much a part of their religious belief and practices as baptism, the confessional, or a sabbath may be for others.

Wisconsin concedes that under the Religion Clauses religious beliefs are absolutely free from the State's control, but it argues that "actions," even though religiously grounded, are outside the protection of the First Amendment. But our decisions have rejected the idea that religiously grounded conduct is always outside the protection of the Free Exercise Clause. It is true that activities of individuals, even when religiously based, are often subject to regulation by the States in the exercise of their undoubted power to promote the health, safety, and general welfare, or the Federal Government in the exercise of its delegated powers. See, e.g., *Gillette* v *United States*, 401 US 437, 28 L Ed 2d 168, 91 S Ct 828 (1971); *Braunfeld* v *Brown*, 366 US 599, 6 L Ed 2d 563, 81 S Ct 1144 (1961); *Prince* v *Massachusetts*, 321 US 158, 88 L Ed 645, 64 S Ct 438 (1944); *Reynolds* v *United States*, 98 US 145, 25 L Ed 244 (1878). But to agree that religiously grounded conduct must often be subject to the broad police power of the State is not to deny that there are areas of conduct protected by the Free Exercise Clause of the First Amendment and thus beyond the power of the State to control, even under regulations of general applicability. E.g., *Sherbert* v *Verner*, 374 US 398, 10 L Ed 2d 965, 83 S Ct 1790 (1963); *Murdock* v *Pennsylvania*, 319 US 105, 87 L Ed 1292, 63 S Ct 870, 146 ALR 81 (1943); *Cantwell* v

Connecticut, 310 US 296, 303-304, 84 L Ed 1213, 1217, 1218, 60 S Ct 900, 128 ALR 1352 (1940). This case, therefore, does not become easier because respondents were convicted for their "actions" in refusing to send their children to the public high school; in this context belief and action cannot be neatly confined in logic-tight compartments. Cf. *Lemon* v *Kurtzman*, 403 US 602, 612, 29 L Ed 2d 745, 755, 91 S Ct 2105 (1971).

Nor can this case be disposed of on the grounds that Wisconsin's requirement for school attendance to age 16 applies uniformly to all citizens of the State and does not, on its face, discriminate against religions or a particular religion, or that it is motivated by legitimate secular concerns. A regulation neutral on its face may, in its application, nonetheless offend the constitutional requirement for governmental neutrality if it unduly burdens the free exercise of religion. *Sherbert* v *Verner*; cf. *Walz* v *Tax Commission*, 397 US 664, 25 L Ed 2d 697, 90 S Ct 1409 (1970). The Court must not ignore the danger that an exception from a general obligation of citizenship on religious grounds may run afoul of the Establishment Clause, but that danger cannot be allowed to prevent any exception no matter how vital it may be to the protection of values promoted by the right of free exercise. By preserving doctrinal flexibility and recognizing the need for a sensible and realistic application of the Religion Clauses "we have been able to chart a course that preserved the autonomy and freedom of religious bodies while avoiding any semblance of established religion. This is a 'tight rope' and one we have successfully traversed." *Walz* v *Tax Commission*, 397 US, at 672, 25 L Ed 2d at 703.

We turn, then, to the State's broader contention that its interest in its system of compulsory education is so compelling that even the established religious practices of the Amish must give way. Where fundamental claims of religious freedom are at stake, however, we cannot accept such a sweeping claim; despite its admitted validity in the generality of cases, we must searchingly examine the interests which the State seeks to promote by its requirement for compulsory education to age 16, and the impediment to those objectives that would flow from recognizing the claimed Amish exemption. See, e.g., *Sherbert* v *Verner*;

Martin v *City of Struthers*, 319 US 141, 87 L Ed 1313, 63 S Ct 862 (1943); *Schneider* v *State*, 308 US 147, 84 L Ed 155, 60 S Ct 146 (1939).

The State advances two primary arguments in support of its system of compulsory education. It notes, as Thomas Jefferson pointed out early in our history, that some degree of education is necessary to prepare citizens to participate effectively and intelligently in our open political system if we are to preserve freedom and independence. Further, education prepares individuals to be self-reliant and self-sufficient participants in society. We accept these propositions.

However, the evidence adduced by the Amish in this case is persuasively to the effect that an additional one or two years of formal high school for Amish children in place of their long established program of informal vocational education would do little to serve those interests. Respondents' experts testified at trial, without challenge, that the value of all education must be assessed in terms of its capacity to prepare the child for life. It is one thing to say that compulsory education for a year or two beyond the eighth grade may be necessary when its goal is the preparation of the child for life in modern society as the majority live, but it is quite another if the goal of education be viewed as the preparation of the child for life in the separated agrarian community that is the keystone of the Amish faith. See *Meyer* v *Nebraska*, 262 US, at 400, 67 L Ed at 1045.

The State attacks respondents' position as one fostering "ignorance" from which the child must be protected by the State. No one can question the State's duty to protect children from ignorance but this argument does not square with the facts disclosed in the record. Whatever their idiosyncrasies as seen by the majority, this record strongly shows that the Amish community has been a highly successful social unit within our society even if apart from the conventional "mainstream." Its members are productive and very law-abiding members of society; they reject public welfare in any of its usual modern forms. The Congress itself recognized their self-sufficiency by authorizing exemption of such groups as the Amish from the obligation to pay social security taxes.

It is neither fair nor correct to suggest that the Amish are opposed to education beyond the eighth grade level. What this record shows is that they are opposed to conventional formal education of the type provided by a certified high school because it comes at the child's crucial adolescent period of religious development. Dr. Donald Erickson, for example, testified that their system of learning-by-doing was an "ideal system" of education in terms of preparing Amish children for life as adults in the Amish community, and that "I would be inclined to say they do a better job in this than most of the rest of us do." As he put it, "these people aren't purporting to be learned people, and it seems to me that the self-sufficiency of the community is the best evidence I can point to—whatever is being done seems to function well."

We must not forget that in the Middle Ages important values of the civilization of the western world were preserved by members of religious orders who isolated themselves from all worldly influences against great obstacles. There can be no assumption that today's majority is "right" and the Amish and others like them are "wrong." A way of life that is odd or even erratic but interferes with no rights or interests of others is not to be condemned because it is different.

The State, however, supports its interest in providing an additional one or two years of compulsory high school education to Amish children because of the possibility that some such children will choose to leave the Amish community, and that if this occurs they will be ill-equipped for life. The State argues that if Amish children leave their church they should not be in the position of making their way in the world without the education available in the one or two additional years the State requires. However, on this record, that argument is highly speculative. There is no specific evidence of the loss of Amish adherents by attrition, nor is there any showing that upon leaving the Amish community Amish children, with their practical agricultural training and habits of industry and self-reliance, would become burdens on society because of educational shortcomings. Indeed, this argument of the State appears to rest primarily on the State's mistaken assumption, already noted, that the Amish do not provide any education for their children beyond the eighth grade, but allow them to grow in "ignorance." To the contrary, not only do the Amish accept the necessity for formal schooling through the eighth grade level, but continue to provide what has been characterized by the undisputed testimony of expert educators as an "ideal" vocational education for their children in the adolescent years.

There is nothing in this record to suggest that the Amish qualities of reliability, self-reliance, and dedication to work would fail to find ready markets in today's society. Absent some contrary evidence supporting the State's position, we are unwilling to assume that persons possessing such valuable vocational skills and habits are doomed to become burdens on society should they determine to leave the Amish faith, nor is there any basis in the record to warrant a finding that an additional one or two years of formal school education beyond the eighth grade would serve to eliminate any such problem that might exist.

Insofar as the State's claim rests on the view that a brief additional period of formal education is imperative to enable the Amish to participate effectively and intelligently in our democratic process, it must fall. The Amish alternative to formal secondary school education has enabled them to function effectively in their day-to-day life under self-imposed limitations on relations with the world, and to survive and prosper in contemporary society as a separate, sharply identifiable and highly self-sufficient community for more than 200 years in this country. In itself this is strong evidence that they are capable of fulfilling the social and political responsibilities of citizenship without compelled attendance beyond the eighth grade at the price of jeopardizing their free exercise of religious belief. When Thomas Jefferson emphasized the need for education as a bulwark of a free people against tyranny, there is nothing to indicate he had in mind compulsory education through any fixed age beyond a basic education. Indeed, the Amish communities singularly parallel and reflect many of the virtues of Jefferson's ideal of the "sturdy yeoman" who would form the basis of what he considered as the ideal of a democratic society. Even their idiosyncratic separateness exemplifies the diversity we profess to admire and encourage.

The requirement for compulsory education beyond the eighth grade is a relatively recent development in our history. Less than 60 years ago, the educational requirements of almost all of the States were satisfied by completion of the elementary grades, at least where the child was regularly and lawfully employed. The independence and successful social functioning of the Amish community for a period approaching almost three centuries and more than 200 years in this country is strong evidence that there is at best a speculative gain, in terms of meeting the duties of citizenship, from an additional one or two years of compulsory formal education. Against this background it would require a more particularized showing from the State on this point to justify the severe interference with religious freedom such additional compulsory attendance would entail.

We should also note that compulsory education and child labor laws find their historical origin in common humanitarian instincts, and that the age limits of both laws have been coordinated to achieve their related objectives. In the context of this case, such considerations, if anything, support rather than detract from respondents' position. The origins of the requirement for school attendance to age 16, an age falling after the completion of elementary school but before completion of high school, are not entirely clear. But to some extent such laws reflected the movement to prohibit most child labor under age 16 that culminated in the provisions of the Federal Fair Labor Standards Act of 1938. It is true, then, that the 16-year child labor age limit may to some degree derive from a contemporary impression that children should be in school until that age. But at the same time, it cannot be denied that, conversely, the 16-year education limit reflects, in substantial measure, the concern that children under that age not be employed under conditions hazardous to their health, or in work that should be performed by adults.

The requirement of compulsory schooling to age 16 must therefore be viewed as aimed not merely at providing educational opportunities for children, but as an alternative to the equally

undesirable consequence of unhealthful child labor displacing
adult workers, or, on the other hand, forced idleness. The two
kinds of statutes—compulsory school attendance and child labor
laws—tend to keep children of certain ages off the labor market
and in school; this in turn provides opportunity to prepare for
a livelihood of a higher order than that children could perform
without education and protects their health in adolescence.

In these terms, Wisconsin's interest in compelling the school
attendance of Amish children to age 16 emerges as somewhat less
substantial than requiring such attendance for children generally.
For, while agricultural employment is not totally outside the
legitimate concerns of the child labor laws, employment of children
under parental guidance and on the family farm from age 14 to
age 16 is an ancient tradition which lies at the periphery of the
objectives of such laws. There is no intimation that the Amish
employment of their children on family farms is in any way
deleterious to their health or that Amish parents exploit children
at tender years. Any such inference would be contrary to the
record before us. Moreover, employment of Amish children on
the family farm does not present the undesirable economic
aspects of eliminating jobs which might otherwise be held by
adults.

IV

Finally, the State, on authority of *Prince* v *Massachusetts*,
argues that a decision exempting Amish children from the State's
requirement fails to recognize the substantive right of the Amish
child to a secondary education, and fails to give due regard
to the power of the State as parens patriae to extend the benefit
of secondary education to children regardless of the wishes of
their parents. Taken at its broadest sweep, the Court's language
in *Prince* might be read to give support to the State's position.
However, the Court was not confronted in *Prince* with a situation
comparable to that of the Amish as revealed in this record;
this is shown by the Court's severe characterization of the evils
which it thought the legislature could legitimately associate with
child labor, even when performed in the company of an adult.
321 US, at 169-170, 88 L Ed at 654. The Court later took

great care to confine Prince to a narrow scope in *Sherbert* v *Verner*, when it stated:

> On the other hand, the Court has rejected challenges
> under the Free Exercise Clause to governmental regulation of
> certain overt acts prompted by religious beliefs or principles,
> for "even when the action is in accord with one's religious
> convictions, [it] is not totally free from legislative
> restrictions." *Braunfeld* v. *Brown*, 366 U.S. 599, 603
> [6 L Ed 2d 563, 566, 81 S Ct 1144]. The conduct or
> actions so regulated have invariably posed some substantial
> threat to public safety, peace or order. See, e.g., *Reynolds*
> v. *United States*, 98 U.S. 145 [25 L Ed 244]; *Jacobson*
> v. *Massachusetts*, 197 U.S. 11 [49 L Ed 643, 25 S Ct 358];
> *Prince* v. *Massachusetts*, 321 U.S. 158 [88 L Ed 645,
> 64 S Ct 438] ... [374 US, at 402-403, 10 L Ed 2d at
> 969, 970].

This case, of course, is not one in which any harm to the
physical or mental health of the child or to the public safety,
peace, order, or welfare has been demonstrated or may be
properly inferred. The record is to the contrary, and any
reliance on that theory would find no support in the evidence.

Contrary to the suggestion of the dissenting opinion of
Mr. Justice Douglas, our holding today in no degree depends on
the assertion of the religious interest of the child as contrasted
with that of the parents. It is the parents who are subject to
prosecution here for failing to cause their children to attend
school, and it is their right of free exercise, not that of their
children, that must determine Wisconsin's power to impose
criminal penalties on the parents. The dissent argues that a
child who expresses a desire to attend public high school in
conflict with the wishes of his parents should not be prevented
from doing so. There is no reason for the Court to consider that
point since it is not an issue in the case. The children are not
parties to this litigation. The State has at no point tried this case
on the theory that respondents were preventing their children
from attending school against their expressed desires, and indeed

the record is to the contrary. The State's position from the outset
has been that it is empowered to apply its compulsory attendance
law to Amish parents in the same manner as to other parents—
that is, without regard to the wishes of the child. That is the
claim we reject today.

Our holding in no way determines the proper resolution of
possible competing interests of parents, children, and the State
in an appropriate state court proceeding in which the power of
the State is asserted on the theory that Amish parents are
preventing their minor children from attending high school
despite their expressed desire to the contrary. Recognition of the
claim of the State in such a proceeding would, of course, call
into question traditional concepts of parental control over the
religious upbringing and education of their minor children
recognized in this Court's past decisions. It is clear that such an
intrusion by a State into family decisions in the area of religious
training would give rise to grave questions of religious freedom
comparable to those raised here and those presented in *Pierce*
v *Society of Sisters.* On this record we neither reach nor decide
those issues.

The State's argument proceeds without reliance on any
actual conflict between the wishes of parents and children.
It appears to rest on the potential that exemption of Amish
parents from the requirements of the compulsory education law
might allow some parents to act contrary to the best interests
of their children by foreclosing their opportunity to make an
intelligent choice between the Amish way of life and that of
the outside world. The same argument could, of course, be made
with respect to all church schools short of college. There is
nothing in the record or in the ordinary course of human
experience to suggest that non-Amish parents generally consult
with children up to ages 14-16 if they are placed in a church
school of the parents' faith.

Indeed it seems clear that if the State is empowered, as
parens patriae, to "save" a child from himself or his Amish parents
by requiring an additional two years of compulsory formal high
school education, the State will in large measure influence, if
not determine, the religious future of the child. Even more

markedly than in *Prince*, therefore, this case involves the fundamental interest of parents, as contrasted with that of the State, to guide the religious future and education of their children. The history and culture of western civilization reflect a strong tradition of parental concern for the nurture and upbringing of their children. This primary role of the parents in the upbringing of their children is now established beyond debate as an enduring American tradition. If not the first, perhaps the most significant statements of the Court in this area are found in *Pierce* v *Society of Sisters*, in which the Court observed:

> Under the doctrine of *Meyer* v. *Nebraska*, 262 U.S. 390, [67 L Ed 1042, 43 S Ct 625, 29 ALR 1446], we think it entirely plain that the Act of 1922 unreasonably interferes with the liberty of parents and guardians to direct the upbringing and education of children under their control. As often heretofore pointed out, rights guaranteed by the Constitution may not be abridged by legislation which has no reasonable relation to some purpose within the competency of the State. The fundamental theory of liberty upon which all governments in this Union repose excludes any general power of the State to standardize its children by forcing them to accept instruction from public teachers only. The child is not the mere creature of the State; those who nurture him and direct his destiny have the right, coupled with the high duty, to recognize and prepare him for additional obligations [268 US, at 534-535, 69 L Ed at 1078].

The duty to prepare the child for "additional obligations," referred to by the Court, must be read to include the inculcation of moral standards, religious beliefs and elements of good citizenship. *Pierce*, of course, recognized that where nothing more than the general interest of the parents in the nurture and education of his children is involved, it is beyond dispute that the State acts "reasonably" and constitutionally in requiring education to age 16 in some public or private school meeting the standards prescribed by the State.

However read, the Court's holding in *Pierce* stands as a charter of the rights of parents to direct the religious upbringing of their children. And, when the interests of parenthood are combined with a free exercise claim of the nature revealed by this record, more than merely a "reasonable relation to some purpose within the competency of the state" is required to sustain the validity of the State's requirement under the First Amendment. To be sure, the power of the parent, even when linked to a free exercise claim, may be subject to limitation under *Prince* if it appears that parental decisions will jeopardize the health or safety of the child, or have a potential for significant social burdens. But in this case, the Amish have introduced persuasive evidence undermining the arguments the State has advanced to support its claims in terms of the welfare of the child and society as a whole. The record strongly indicates that accommodating the religious objections of the Amish by forgoing one, or at most two, additional years of compulsory education will not impair the physical or mental health of the child, nor result in an inability to be self-supporting, or to discharge the duties and responsibilities of citizenship, or in any other way materially detract from the welfare of society.

In the face of our consistent emphasis on the central values underlying the Religion Clauses in our constitutional scheme of government, we cannot accept a parens patriae claim of such all-encompassing scope and with such sweeping potential for broad and unforeseeable application as that urged by the State.

V

For the reasons stated we hold, with the Supreme Court of Wisconsin, that the First and Fourteenth Amendments prevent the State from compelling respondents to cause their children to attend formal high school to age 16. Our disposition of this case, however, in no way alters our recognition of the obvious fact that courts are not school boards or legislatures, and are ill-equipped to determine the "necessity" of discrete aspects of a State's program of compulsory education. This should suggest that courts must move with great circumspection in performing the sensitive and delicate task of weighing a State's legitimate social concern when faced with religious claims for exemption from generally applicable educational requirements. It cannot be over-emphasized that we are not dealing with a way of life and mode of education by a group claiming to have recently discovered some "progressive" or more enlightened process for rearing children for modern life.

Aided by a history of three centuries as an identifiable religious sect and a long history as a successful and self-sufficient segment of American society, the Amish in this case have convincingly demonstrated the sincerity of their religious beliefs, the interrelationship of belief with their mode of life, the vital role which belief and daily conduct play in the continued survival of Old Order Amish communities and their religious organization, and the hazards presented by the State's enforcement of a statute generally valid as to others. Beyond this, they have carried the even more difficult burden of demonstrating the adequacy of their alternative mode of continuing informal vocational education in terms of precisely those overall interests that the State advances in support of its program of compulsory high school education. In light of this convincing showing, one which probably few other religious groups or sects could make, and weighing the minimal difference between what the State would require and what the Amish already accept, it was incumbent on the State to show with more particularity how its admittedly strong interest in compulsory education would be adversely affected by granting an exemption to the Amish. *Sherbert* v *Verner.*

Nothing we hold is intended to undermine the general applicability of the State's compulsory school attendance statutes or to limit the power of the State to promulgate reasonable standards that, while not impairing the free exercise of religion, provide for continuing agricultural vocational education under parental and church guidance by the Old Order Amish or others similarly situated. The States have had a long history of amicable and effective relationships with church-sponsored schools, and there is no basis for assuming that in this related context, reasonable standards cannot be established concerning the content of the continuing vocational education of Amish children under parental guidance, provided always that state regulations are not inconsistent with what we have said in this opinion.

Affirmed.

Mr. Justice Powell and Mr. Justice Rehnquist took no part in the consideration or decision of this case.

SEPARATE OPINIONS

Mr. Justice Stewart, with whom Mr. Justice Brennan joins, concurring.

This case involves the constitutionality of imposing criminal punishment upon Amish parents for their religiously based refusal to compel their children to attend public high schools. Wisconsin has sought to brand these parents as criminals for following their religious beliefs, and the Court today rightly holds that Wisconsin cannot constitutionally do so.

This case in no way involves any questions regarding the right of the children of Amish parents to attend public high schools, or any other institutions of learning, if they wish to do so. As the Court points out, there is no suggestion whatever in the record that the religious beliefs of the children here concerned differ in any way from those of their parents. Only one of the children testified. The last two questions and answers on her cross-examination accurately sum up her testimony.

"Q. So I take it then, Frieda, the only reason you are not going to school, and did not go to school since last September, is because of your religion?

"A. Yes.

"Q. That is the only reason?

"A. Yes."

It is clear to me, therefore, that this record simply does not present the interesting and important issue discussed in Part II of the dissenting opinion of Mr. Justice Douglas. With this observation, I join the opinion and the judgment of the Court.

Mr. Justice White, with whom Mr. Justice Brennan and Mr. Justice Stewart join, concurring.

Cases such as this one inevitably call for a delicate balancing of important but conflicting interests. I join the opinion and judgment of the Court because I cannot say that the State's interest in requiring two more years of compulsory education in the ninth and tenth grades outweighs the importance of the concededly sincere Amish religious practice to the survival of that sect.

This would be a very different case for me if respondents' claim were that their religion forbade their children from attending any school at any time and from complying in any way with the educational standards set by the State. Since the Amish children are permitted to acquire the basic tools of literacy to survive in modern society by attending grades one through eight and since the deviation from the State's compulsory education law is relatively slight, I conclude that respondents' claim must prevail, largely because "religious freedom—the freedom to believe and to practice strange and, it may be, foreign creeds—has classically been one of the highest values of our society." *Braunfeld* v *Brown*, 366 US 599, 612, 6 L Ed 2d 563, 571, 81 S Ct 1144 (1961) (Brennan, J., dissenting).

The importance of the state interest asserted here cannot be denigrated, however:

> Today, education is perhaps the most important function of state and local governments. Compulsory school attendance laws and the great expenditures for education both demonstrate our recognition of the importance of education to our democratic society. It is required in the performance of our most basic public responsibilities, even service in the armed forces. It is the very foundation of good citizenship. Today it is a principal instrument in awakening the child to cultural values, in preparing him for later professional training, and in helping him to adjust normally to his environment [*Brown* v *Board of Education*, 347 US 483, 493, 98 L Ed 873, 880, 74 S Ct 686, 38 ALR 2d 1180 (1954)].

As recently as last Term, the Court re-emphasized the legitimacy of the State's concern for enforcing minimal educational standards, *Lemon* v *Kurtzman,* 403 US 602, 613, 29 L Ed 2d 745, 755,

91 S Ct 2105 (1971). *Pierce v Society of Sisters*, 268 US 510, 69 L Ed 1070, 45 S Ct 571, 39 ALR 468 (1925), lends no support to the contention that parents may replace state educational requirements with their own idiosyncratic views of what knowledge a child needs to be a productive and happy member of society; in Pierce, both the parochial and military schools were in compliance with all the educational standards which the State had set, and the Court held simply that while a State may posit such standards, it may not pre-empt the educational process by requiring children to attend public schools. In the present case, the State is not concerned with the maintenance of an educational system as an end in itself, it is rather attempting to nurture and develop the human potential of its children, whether Amish or non-Amish: to expand their knowledge, broaden their sensibilities, kindle their imagination, foster a spirit of free inquiry, and increase their human understanding and tolerance. It is possible that most Amish children will wish to continue living the rural life of their parents, in which case their training at home will adequately equip them for their future role. Others, however, may wish to become nuclear physicists, ballet dancers, computer programmers, or historians, and for these occupations, formal training will be necessary. There is evidence in the record that many children desert the Amish faith when they come of age. A State has a legitimate interest not only in seeking to develop the latent talents of its children but in seeking to prepare them for the life style which they may later choose or at least to provide them with an option other than the life they have led in the past. In the circumstances of this case, although the question is close, I am unable to say that the State has demonstrated that Amish children who leave school in the eighth grade will be intellectually stultified or unable to acquire new academic skills later. The statutory minimum school attendance age set by the State is, after all, only 16.

Decision in cases such as this and the administration of an exemption for Old Order Amish from the State's compulsory school attendance laws will inevitably involve the kind of close and perhaps repeated scrutiny of religious practices, as exemplified

in today's opinion, which the Court has heretofore been anxious
to avoid. But such entanglement does not create a forbidden
establishment of religion where it is essential to implement
free exercise values threatened by an otherwise neutral program
instituted to foster some permissible, nonreligious state objective.
I join the Court because the sincerity of the Amish religious
policy here is uncontested, because the potential adverse impact
of the state requirement is great and because the State's valid
interest in education has already been largely satisfied by the
eight years the children have already spent in school.

Mr. Justice Douglas, dissenting in part.

I

I agree with the Court that the religious scruples of the
Amish are opposed to the education of their children beyond the
grade schools, yet I disagree with the Court's conclusion that
the matter is within the dispensation of parents alone. The Court's
analysis assumes that the only interests at stake in the case
are those of the Amish parents on the one hand, and those of
the State on the other. The difficulty with this approach is that,
despite the Court's claim, the parents are seeking to vindicate
not only their own free exercise claims, but also those of their
high-school-age children.

It is argued that the right of the Amish children to religious
freedom is not presented by the facts of the case, as the issue
before the Court involves only the Amish parents' religious freedom
to defy a state criminal statute imposing upon them an affirmative
duty to cause their children to attend high school.

First, respondents' motion to dismiss in the trial court
expressly asserts, not only the religious liberty of the adults,
but also that of the children, as a defense to the prosecutions.
It is, of course, beyond question that the parents have standing
as defendants in a criminal prosecution to assert the religious
interests of their children as a defense. Although the lower courts
and the majority in this Court assume an identity of interest
between parent and child, it is clear that they have treated the
religious interest of the child as a factor in the analysis.

Second, it is essential to reach the question to decide the

case not only because the question was squarely raised in the motion to dismiss, but also because no analysis of religious liberty claims can take place in a vacuum. If the parents in this case are allowed a religious exemption, the inevitable effect is to impose the parents' notions of religious duty upon their children. Where the child is mature enough to express potentially conflicting desires, it would be an invasion of the child's rights to permit such an imposition without canvassing his views. As in *Prince*, it is an imposition resulting from this very litigation. As the child has no other effective forum, it is in this litigation that his rights should be considered. And, if an Amish child desires to attend high school, and is mature enough to have that desire respected, the State may well be able to override the parents' religiously motivated objections.

Religion is an individual experience. It is not necessary, nor even appropriate, for every Amish child to express his views on the subject in a prosecution of a single adult. Crucial, however, are the views of the child whose parent is the subject of the suit. Frieda Yoder has in fact testified that her own religious views are opposed to high-school education. I therefore join the judgment of the Court as to respondent Jonas Yoder. But Frieda Yoder's views may not be those of Vernon Yutzy or Barbara Miller. I must dissent, therefore, as to respondents Adin Yutzy and Wallace Miller as their motion to dismiss also raised the question of their children's religious liberty.

II

This issue has never been squarely presented before today. Our opinions are full of talk about the power of the parents over the child's education. See *Pierce* v *Society of Sisters*, 268 US 510, 69 L Ed 1070, 45 S Ct 571, 39 ALR 468; *Meyer* v *Nebraska*, 262 US 390, 67 L Ed 1042, 43 S Ct 625, 29 ALR 1446. And we have in the past analyzed similar conflicts between parent and State with little regard for the views of the child. See *Prince* v *Massachusetts*, 321 US 158, 88 L Ed 645, 64 S Ct 438. Recent cases, however, have clearly held that the children themselves have constitutionally protectible interests.

These children are "persons" within the meaning of the

Bill of Rights. We have so held over and over again. In *Haley* v *Ohio*, 332 US 596, 92 L Ed 224, 68 S Ct 302, we extended the protection of the Fourteenth Amendment in a state trial of a 15-year-old boy. In *In re Gault*, 387 US 1, 13, 18 L Ed 2d 527, 538, 87 S Ct 1428, we held that "neither the Fourteenth Amendment nor the Bill of Rights is for adults alone." In *In re Winship*, 397 US 358, 25 L Ed 2d 368, 90 S Ct 1068, we held that a 12-year-old boy, when charged with an act which would be a crime if committed by an adult, was entitled to procedural safeguards contained in the Sixth Amendment.

In *Tinker* v *Des Moines School District*, 393 US 503, 21 L Ed 2d 731, 89 S Ct 733, we dealt with 13-year-old, 15-year-old, and 16-year-old students who wore armbands to public schools and were disciplined for doing so. We gave them relief, saying that their First Amendment rights had been abridged.

> Students in school as well as out of school are "persons" under our Constitution. They are possessed of fundamental rights which the State must respect, just as they themselves must respect the obligations to the State [Id., at 511, 21 L Ed 2d at 740].

In *Board of Education* v *Barnette*, 319 US 624, 87 L Ed 1628, 63 S Ct 1178, 147 ALR 674, we held that school children, whose religious beliefs collided with a school rule requiring them to salute the flag, would not be required to do so. While the sanction included expulsion of the students and prosecution of the parents, id., at 630, 87 L Ed at 1633, the vice of the regime was its interference with the child's free exercise of religion. We said: "Here . . . we are dealing with a compulsion of students to declare a belief" [Id., at 631, 87 L Ed at 1634]. In emphasizing the important and delicate tasks of boards of education we said:

> . . . That they are educating the young for citizenship is reason for scrupulous protection of Constitutional freedoms of the individual, if we are not to strangle the free mind at its source and teach youth to discount important principles of our government as mere platitudes.

On this important and vital matter of education, I think the children should be entitled to be heard. While the parents, absent dissent, normally speak for the entire family, the education of the child is a matter on which the child will often have decided views. He may want to be a pianist or an astronaut or an ocean geographer. To do so he will have to break from the Amish tradition.

It is the future of the student, not the future of the parents, that is imperiled in today's decision. If a parent keeps his child out of school beyond the grade school, then the child will be forever barred from entry into the new and amazing world of diversity that we have today. The child may decide that that is the preferred course, or he may rebel. It is the student's judgment, not his parent's, that is essential if we are to give full meaning to what we have said about the Bill of Rights and of the right of students to be masters of their own destiny. If he is harnessed to the Amish way of life by those in authority over him and if his education is truncated, his entire life may be stunted and deformed. The child, therefore, should be given an opportunity to be heard before the State gives the exemption which we honor today.

The views of the two children in question were not canvassed by the Wisconsin courts. The matter should be explicitly reserved so that new hearings can be held on remand of the case.

III

I think the emphasis of the Court on the "law and order" record of this Amish group of people is quite irrelevant. A religion is a religion irrespective of what the misdemeanor or felony records of its members might be. I am not at all sure how the Catholics, Episcopalians, the Baptists, Jehovah's Witnesses, the Unitarians, and my own Presbyterians would make out if we were subjected to such a test. It is, of course, true that if a group or society was organized to perpetuate crime and if that is its motif, we would have rather startling problems akin to those that were raised when some years back a particular sect was challenged here as operating on a fraudulent basis.

United States v *Ballard*, 322 US 78, 88 L Ed 1148, 64 S Ct 882.
But no such factors are present here, and the Amish, whether with
a high or low criminal record, certainly qualify by all historic
standards as a religion within the meaning of the First Amendment.

The Court rightly rejects the notion that actions, even though
religiously grounded, are outside the protection of the Free
Exercise Clause of the First Amendment. In so ruling, the Court
departs from the teaching of *Reynolds* v *United States*, 98 US 145,
164, 25 L Ed 244, 250, where it was said concerning the reach
of the Free Exercise Clause of the First Amendment, "Congress
was deprived of all legislative power over mere opinion, but was
left free to reach actions which were in violation of social duties
or subversive of good order." In that case it was conceded that
polygamy was a part of the religion of the Mormons. Yet the
Court said, "It matters not that his belief (in polygamy) was a
part of his professed religion; it was still belief and only belief"
[Id., at 167, 25 L Ed at 250].

Action, which the Court deemed to be antisocial, could be
punished even though it was grounded on deeply held and
sincere religious convictions. What we do today, at least in this
respect, opens the way to give organized religion a broader base
than it has ever enjoyed; and it even promises that in time
Reynolds will be overruled.

In another way, however, the Court retreats when in
reference to Henry Thoreau it says his "choice was philosophical
and personal rather than religious, and such belief does not rise
to the demands of the Religion Clause." That is contrary to what
we held in *United States* v *Seeger*, 380 US 163, 13 L Ed 2d 733,
85 S Ct 850, where we were concerned with the meaning of
the words "religious training and belief" in the Selective Service
Act, which were the basis of many conscientious objector claims.
We said:

> . . . Within that phrase would come all sincere religious
> beliefs which are based upon a power or being, or upon a
> faith, to which all else is subordinate or upon which all else is
> ultimately dependent. The test might be stated in these words:
> A sincere and meaningful belief which occupies in the life of

its possessor a place parallel to that filled by the God of
those admittedly qualifying for the exemption comes within
the statutory definition. This construction avoids imputing to
Congress an intent to classify different religious beliefs,
exempting some and excluding others, and is in accord
with the well-established congressional policy of equal
treatment for those whose opposition to service is grounded
in their religious tenets [Id., 176, 13 L Ed 2d at 743].

Welsh v *United States*, 398 US 333, 26 L Ed 2d 308,
90 S Ct 1792, was in the same vein, the Court saying:

> . . . In this case, Welsh's conscientious objection to war
> was undeniably based in part on his perception of world
> politics. In a letter to his local board, he wrote:
> "I can only act according to what I am and what I
> see. And I see that the military complex wastes both human
> and material resources, that it fosters disregard for (what I
> consider a paramount concern) human needs and ends;
> I see that the means we employ to 'defend' our 'way of life'
> profoundly change that way of life. I see that in our failure
> to recognize the political, social, and economic realities of
> the world, we, as a nation, fail our responsibility as a nation"
> [Id., 342, 26 L Ed 2d at 320].

The essence of Welsh's philosophy on the basis of which we
held he was entitled to an exemption was in these words:

> I believe that human life is valuable in and of itself;
> in its living; therefore I will not injure or kill another
> human being. This belief (and the corresponding "duty" to
> abstain from violence toward another person) is not "superior
> to those arising from any human relation." On the contrary:
> it is essential to every human relation. I cannot, therefore,
> conscientiously comply with the Government's insistence
> that I assume duties which I feel are immoral and totally
> repugnant [Id., 343, 26 L Ed 2d at 320].

I adhere to these exalted views of "religion" and see no acceptable alternative to them now that we have become a Nation of many religions and sects, representing all of the diversities of the human race. 380 US, at 192-193, 13 L Ed 2d at 751, 752.

Notes

1 FROM ERLANBACH TO NEW GLARUS

1. Quoted in Stephen Arons, "Compulsory Education: The Plain People People Resist," *Saturday Review* (January 15, 1972), p. 55.

2. John A Hostetler, "Old World Extinction and New World Survival of the Amish: A Study of Group Maintenance and Dissolution," *Rural Sociology* (September-December, 1955), p. 212ff.

3. Harold S. Bender, "Some Early American Amish-Mennonite Disciplines," *Mennonite Quarterly Review*, 8 (April, 1934), p. 95ff.

4. Ibid.

5. David V. Treyer, *Hinterlassene Schriften* (Arthur, Illinois: L. A. Miller, 1925), pp. 56-57.

6. John Umble, ed., "Memoirs of An Amish Bishop," *Mennonite Quarterly Review*, 22 (April, 1948), p. 102.

7. *Herald der Wahrheit* (July 1, 1882).

8. Samuel D. Guengerich, *Deutsche Gemeinde Schulen* (Amish, Iowa: published by the author, 1897), p. 7.

9. Robert H. Bremner, et al., eds., *Children and Youth in America: 1866-1932,* 2 (Cambridge: Harvard University Press, 1971), p. 421.

10. Richard Hofstadter, *Anti-Intellectualism in American Life* (New York: Vintage Books, 1966), p. 325.

11. Raymond E. Callahan, *An Introduction to Education in American Society* (New York: Alfred A. Knopf, 1961), p. 141.

12. Robert J. Alley, "The Consolidation of Schools," *National Education Association Journal of Proceedings and Addresses* (July 2-8, 1910), p. 277.

13. *Wooster Daily Record* (March 28, 1958).

14. *The Budget* (November 6, 1952).

15. *Geauga County Record* (December 17, 1915).

2 WHO SHALL EDUCATE OUR CHILDREN?

1. William R. McGrath, *The Budget* (June 3, 1965).

2. Quoted by Stephen M. Stoltzfus, "Why a Christian Day School Today?," Smith-Peloubt Bible Dictionary.

3. John Horsch, *Mennonites in Europe* (Scottdale, Pennsylvania: Mennonite Publishing House, 1942), p. 5.

4. Ibid., p. 229.

5. Quoted by Elder A. Goerz, *Mennonite Encyclopedia* (Hillsboro, Kansas: Mennonite Brethren Publishing House, 1955), 2, p. 154.

6. A Brother, *Herold der Wahrheit* (July 1, 1882).

7. Samuel D. Guengerich, *Deutsche Gemeinder Schulen* (Amish, Iowa: published by the author, 1897).

8. Abraham S. Yoder, *My Life Story* (1965), p. 12.

9. Ibid., p. 15.

10. Ibid., p. 18.

11. *Complete Writings of Menno Simons* (Scottdale, Pennsylvania: Mennonite Publishing House, 1956), p. 950.

12. Marianne Brown, *Gospel Herald* (August 8, 1961).

13. *Menno Simons*, p. 951.

14. C. D. and M. D. Esch, *Christian Standards of Social Purity* (1931).

15. Orrie D. Yoder, "Unique Privileges of our Christian Schools," *Sword and Trumpet* (First Quarter, 1962).

16. Donalda Dickie, *The Great Adventure* (Toronto: Dent Publishing Company, 1958).

17. *Ontario Elementary School Radio Broadcasts, 1965-66*, p. 61.

18. C. D. and M. D. Esch, *Christian Standards*.

19. Robert R. Rusk, *Doctrines of the Great Educators* (Melbourne: Macmillan, 1969), p. 287.

20. Editorial, "Strong Delusion," *The Blackboard Bulletin*, 6, No. 9.

21. As reprinted in "The King's Business" and quoted in *Doctrines of the Bible*, Daniel Kauffman (Scottdale, Pennsylvania: Mennonite Publishing House, 1928), p. 234.

22. Ibid., p. 232.

23. *The Educational Courier* (July, 1961).

24. Helen Worthington, "An Organized Routine for Russian Babies," *The Toronto Telegram* (June 16, 1965).

25. "The Need for Christian Day Schools," *Gospel Herald* (August 8, 1961).

4 THE PERSECUTION OF LEROY GARBER

1. Paper presented at the Conference on Child Socialization, Temple University, Philadelphia, March 21, 1969.

I am indebted to the Danforth Foundation for financial support of the research on which this paper is based. However, the foundation should not be held responsible for viewpoints expressed here.

2. In preparation for this paper I conducted sixty personal interviews, averaging slightly more than forty-five minutes each, with sixty-seven individuals who were qualified to shed light on the Garber incident; and I interviewed an additional six individuals by telephone. The interviews were held, and other data gathered, on four trips to Kansas between November 28, 1967 and February 5, 1968.

3. For a more comprehensive discussion of Amish educational practice and its defensibility, see Donald A. Erickson, "The Plain People vs. the Common Schools," *Saturday Review*, November 19, 1966, pp. 83-87, 102-3; and Donald A. Erickson, ed., *Public Controls for Nonpublic Schools* (Chicago: University of Chicago Press, 1969).

4. Sharon L. Garber, "Letter from Sharon," *Family Life* (March, 1968), pp. 18-19.

5. L. A. Noll (curriculum director, Hutchinson Public Schools), who administered the GED in south-central Kansas from 1947 to 1967, could not remember a single college-age Amishman or other member of a bearded Mennonite group who failed to pass the GED. Both he and the college officers whom I interviewed or contacted by correspondence reported the tendency for Plain People who were admitted to colleges on the basis of the GED to make above-average records. In an effort to secure more objective evidence on this point, I conducted the following inquiry:

According to my interviews, almost all Plain People who entered colleges on the basis of scores on the GED attended Bethel College, a Mennonite institution in North Newton, Kansas; Hesston College, a Mennonite institution in Hesston, Kansas; McPherson College, a Church of the Brethren college in McPherson, Kansas; Hutchinson Community Junior College, a public institution in Hutchinson, Kansas; and Wichita State University, a public institution in Wichita, Kansas. In conversations with officials at the Hutchinson Community Junior College, I was advised that admissions officers in small Kansas colleges would probably be able to compile lists of Plain People admitted during the past ten years on the basis of scores on the GED, since these students are relatively few and are usually watched with unusual interest. I wrote to each of the above-mentioned colleges, requesting that such a list be supplied to me for research purposes. Only Wichita State University replied that it was not feasible to obtain such information from existing records. Four names and addresses were provided by Bethel College, eight from Hesston College, two from McPherson College, and nine from Hutchinson Community Junior College, for a total of twenty-three. Since two students were reported by two different colleges, only twenty-one different individuals were involved. I wrote to each of these students individually, explaining the nature of the research and requesting that they request the respective colleges to send me transcripts (at no cost to the students, through arrangements I made with the colleges) of their academic records. One individual responded with information that she had never taken any courses at the college that provided her name, and my letter to another individual was returned marked "addressee unknown." Follow-up letters were sent to all individuals who did not respond within five weeks. Of the nineteen who had taken courses in the colleges in question and who apparently received my request, sixteen (84 percent) responded by having the college send me their transcripts. The academic records of the sixteen respondents, as reported in these transcripts, are summarized below (see table).

Academic Achievement of Sixteen Respondents Admitted to Four Kansas Colleges on Basis of GED

Respondent	No. of Courses Completed	Grade-Point Average	Letter-Grade Average
a	1	2.00	C
b	1	2.00	C
c	1	3.00	B
d	3	3.67	A
e	5	2.80	B
f	7	2.86	B
g	11	2.91	B
h	11	3.00	B
i	16	2.75	B
j	20	3.78	A
k	23	2.74	B
l	23	2.71	B
m	23	2.11	C
n	28	3.82	A
o	36	3.00	B
p	38	3.85	A

For present purposes, the grade-point average was calculated by allotting a value of 4 to a grade of A, 3 to a grade of B, 2 to a grade of C, and 1 to a grade of D (no lower grades were recorded for the group), summing the values for all such letter grades (excluding grades of S, P, etc., for which no value could be logically assigned), and dividing the sum by the number of courses for which such grades had been indicated. The letter average was obtained by rounding the quotient to the nearest whole number and recording the corresponding letter grade.

Respondents *d* and *o*, who had also attended colleges I did not contact in this inquiry, including two out-of-state colleges, voluntarily asked these other colleges to send me academic transcripts. When the additional data are considered, respondent *d* is seen to have completed thirty-five courses in all, with a grade-point average slightly lower than formerly (3.18 instead of 3.67); and respondent *o* is seen to have completed a total of fifty courses, with a grade-point average somewhat higher than formerly (3.02 instead of 3.00). These very limited data do not support the likelihood that the four Kansas colleges from which the main body of data were obtained are unusually lenient in their grading policies.

6. Erickson, *Public Controls for Nonpublic Schools*, pp. 15-48.
7. W. H. Auden, "Musée des Beaux Arts."

6   THE CULTURAL CONTEXT OF THE WISCONSIN CASE

1. Donald A. Erickson, ed., *Public Controls for Nonpublic Schools* (Chicago: University of Chicago Press, 1969). See Ch. 2, "Showdown at an Amish Schoolhouse: A Description and Analysis of the Iowa Controversy."

2. Dan M. Borntreger of Iowa wrote to the National Committee for Amish Religious Freedom on May 19, 1969: ". . . remember if you lose, things will be worse."

3. For greater elaboration of the basic beliefs see J. A. Hostetler, *Amish Society* (Baltimore: Johns Hopkins University Press, 1968), pp. 47-69.

4. Franklin H. Littell, "Sectarian Protestantism and the Pursuit of Wisdom: Must Technological Objectives Prevail?," *Public Controls for Nonpublic Schools*, p. 65.

5. Charles P. Loomis and J. Allan Beegle, *Rural Social Systems* (Englewood Cliffs, N. J.: Prentice-Hall, 1957), pp. 590-91.

6. John A. Hostetler and Gertrude E. Huntington, *Children in Amish Society: Socialization and Community Education* (New York: Holt Rinehart and Winston, 1971), pp. 80-96.

7. The personality type of the Amish is based on the use of the Myers Briggs Indicator. See ibid., pp. 80-82.

8. Jeffrey W. Kobrick, "The Compelling Case for Bilingual Education," *Saturday Review* (April 29, 1972), p. 57.

9. Quotation from a pamphlet by Benjamin Franklin, ca. 1784, "Remarks Concerning the Savages of North America," in Everett Reiner, *School Is Dead: Alternatives of Education* (New York: Anchor Books, 1972), p. 37.

Bibliography

I. BOOKS:

Antieau, C. J., P. M. Carroll, and T. C. Burke, *Religion Under the State Constitutions* (Brooklyn: Central Book Company, 1965).

Bachman, Calvin George, *The Old Order Amish of Lancaster County* (Norristown, Pennsylvania: Proceedings of the Pennsylvania German Society, 1942), reprinted 1961.

Beachy, Alvin, *The Amish of Somerset County, Pennsylvania: A Study in the Rise and Development of the Beachy Amish Mennonite Churches* (Hartford, Connecticut: Hartford Seminary Foundation, 1952).

Beiler, Aaron E., ed., *Records of Principles Pertaining to the Old Order Amish Church Sect School Committee as of September 2, 1937*, reaffirmed and approved through counsel of the committee, August 9, 1961 (Gap, Pennsylvania: School Committee, 1961).

Blanshard, Paul, *Religion and the Schools: The Great Controversy* (Boston: Beacon Press, 1963).

Boles, Donald, *The Bible, Religion and the Public Schools* (Ames, Iowa: Iowa State University, 1961).

Bower, William Clayton, *Moral and Spiritual Values in Education* (Lexington, Kentucky: University of Kentucky Press, 1952).

Braght, Thieleman J. van, *The Bloody Theatre or Martyrs Mirror of the Defenseless Christians Who Baptized Only Upon Confession of Faith, and Who Suffered and Died for the Testimony of Jesus, Their Saviour, From the Time of Christ to the Year A.D. 1660* (Scottdale, Pennsylvania: Mennonite Publishing House, 1950).

Bremmer, Robert, *Children and Youth in America: A Documentary History* (Cambridge, Massachusetts: Harvard University Press, 1971).

Brickman, William W. and Stanley Lehrer, eds., *Religion, Government and Education* (New York: Society for the Advancement of Education, 1961).

Brown, Samuel W., *The Secularization of American Education as Shown by State Legislation, State Constitutional Provisions and State Supreme Court Decisions* (New York: Columbia University, 1912).

Byler, Uria R., *School Bells Ringing: A Manual for Amish Teachers and Parents* (Aylmer, Ontario, Canada: Pathway Publishing Corporation, 1969).

Callahan, Raymond E., *Education and the Cult of Efficiency* (Chicago: University of Chicago Press, 1962).

Cavell, Jean Moore, *Religious Education Among People of Germanic Origin in Colonial Pennsylvania* (Norristown, Pennsylvania: The Pennsylvania German Society, 1929).

Cogley, John, ed., *Religion in America* (Cleveland: World Publishing Company, 1968).

Cremin, Lawrence, *The Transformation of the School: Progressivism in American Education 1867-1957* (New York: Alfred A. Knopf, 1961).

Dahl, John A., Marvin Lasser, Robert Cathbert, and Fred Marcus, eds., *Student, School, and Society* (San Francisco: Chandler Publishing Company, 1965).

Dierenfield, Richard B., *Religion in American Public Schools* (Washington, D.C.: Public Affairs Press, 1962).

Douglas, William O., *The Bible and the Schools* (Boston: Little, Brown, 1966).

Drinan, Robert F., *Religion, the Courts, and Public Policy* (New York: McGraw-Hill, 1963).

Drouin, Edmund G., ed., *The School Question: A Bibliography on Church-State Relationships in American Education 1940-1960* (Washington, D.C.: The Catholic University of America Press, 1963).

Dunn, William Kailer, *What Happened to Religious Education? The Decline of Religious Teaching in the Public Elementary School, 1776-1861* (Baltimore: Johns Hopkins University Press, 1958).

Erickson, Donald A., ed., *Public Controls for Nonpublic Schools* (Chicago: University of Chicago Press, 1969).

Fichter, Joseph H., *Parochial Schools: A Sociological Study* (Notre Dame: University of Notre Dame Press, 1958).

Fleming, W. S., *God in Our Public Schools* (Pittsburgh: National Reform Association, 1947).

Forbes, Jack D., *The Education of the Culturally Different, A Multi-Cultural Approach* (Berkeley: The Far Western Laboratory for Educational Research and Development, 1951).

Francis, Emerick K., *In Search of Utopia: The Mennonites in Manitoba* (Glencoe: Free Press, 1955).

Freund, Paul A., and Robert Ulich, *Religion and the Public Schools* (Cambridge: Harvard University Press, 1965).

Friedenberg, Edgar Z., *Coming of Age in America: Growth and Acquiescence* (New York: Random House, 1963).

Gesell, A. and F. Ilg, *Youth: The Years from Ten to Sixteen* (New York: Harper, 1956).

Giannella, Donald A., ed., *Religion and the Public Order, 1964* (Chicago: University of Chicago Press, 1965).

Gingerich, Ervin, *Ohio Amish Directory* (Plain City, Ohio, 1959, 1960).

Goodman, Paul, *Compulsory Miseducation* (New York: Horizon Press, 1964).

Guengerich, Samuel D., *Deutsche Gemeinde Schulen* (Amish, Iowa: published by the author, 1897).

Hartford, E. F., *Moral Values in Public Education: Lessons from the Kentucky Experience* (New York: Harper, 1958).

Hartzler, John E., *Education Among the Mennonites of America* (Danvers, Illinois: The Central Mennonite Publishing Board, 1925).

Hayes, Reed, Jr., *The Old Order Amish Mennonites of Pennsylvania, A Survival of Religious Fundamentalism in a New World Environment* (Lewistown, Pennsylvania: Mifflin County Historical Society, 1946).

Henry, Jules, *Culture Against Man* (New York: Random House, 1963).

Henry, Virgil, *The Place of Religion in the Public Schools* (New York: Harper, 1950).

Hershberger, Henry J., *Minimum Standards for the Amish Parochial or Private Elementary Schools of the State of Ohio as a Form of Regulation: Compiled and Approved by Bishops, Committeemen and Others in Conference* (Apple Creek, Ohio: published by the author, 1960).

Hershberger, Jacob J., ed., *Our Youths: A Collection of Letters Pertaining to the Conditions Among Our Youth, The Amish Mennonites* (Lynnhaven, Virginia: published by the author, 1955).

Horsch, John, *Mennonites in Europe* (Scottdale, Pennsylvania: Mennonite Publishing House, 1942).

Hostetler, John A., *Annotated Bibliography on the Amish* (Scottdale, Pennsylvania: Mennonite Publishing House, 1951).

————, *Amish Society* (Baltimore: Johns Hopkins University Press, 1963).

————, *Conference on Child Socialization* (Washington, D.C.: U.S. Department of Health, Education, and Welfare, 1969).

————, *Educational Achievements and Life Styles in a Traditional Society, the Old Order Amish* (Washington, D.C.: U.S. Department of Health, Education, and Welfare, 1969).

Hostetler, John A., and Gertrude Enders Huntington, *Children in Amish Society: Socialization and Community Education* (New York: Holt, Rinehart, and Winston, 1971).

Johnson, F. Ernest, ed., *American Education and Religion* (New York: Harper, 1952).

Katz, Wilber, *Religion and American Constitutions* (Evanston, Illinois: Northwestern University Press, 1964).

Kauper, Paul G., *Religion and the Constitution* (Baton Rouge: Louisiana State University Press, 1964).

Kollmorgen, Walter M., *Culture of a Contemporary Rural Community: The Old Order Amish of Lancaster County, Pennsylvania*, Rural Life Studies: 4 (Washington, D.C.: U.S. Department of Agriculture, September, 1942).

Kurland, Philip B., *Religion and the Law: Of Church and State and the Supreme Court* (Chicago: Aldine, 1962).

Loughery, M. Bernard Francis, *Parental Rights in American Educational Law: Their Bases and Implementation* (Washington, D.C.: Catholic University, 1952).

Manwaring, David, *Render Unto Caesar—The Flag-Salute Controversy* (Chicago: University of Chicago Press, 1962).

Mast, Daniel E., *Salvation Full and Free* (Inman, Kansas: Salem Publishing House, 1955).

Mast, John B., ed., *Eine Erklärung über Bann und Meidung Geschrieben zur zeit der Amisch Spalt von 1693-1711* (1949).

————, ed., *The Letters of the Amish Division* (Oregon City, Oregon: Christian J. Schlabaugh, 1950).

Mennonite Encyclopedia (Scottdale, Pennsylvania: Mennonite
    Publishing House; Hillsboro, Kansas: Mennonite Brethren
    Publishing House; North Newton, Kansas: Mennonite
    Publication Office, 1956-59), 4 vols.
Miller, Edward A., *The History of Educational Legislation in
    Ohio from 1803-1850* (Chicago: University of Chicago, 1920).
Miller, Elizabeth M., *From the Fiery Stakes of Europe to the
    Federal Courts of America* (New York: Vintage Press, 1963).
Miller, L. A., ed., *Handbuch für Prediger* (Arthur, Illinois:
    published by the author, 1950).
*Minimum Standards for the Amish Parochial and Vocational
    Schools of the State of Pennsylvania* (Gordonville,
    Pennsylvania: Old Order Book Society, 1969).
Moehlman, Conrad H., *The Church as Educator* (New York: Hinds,
    Hayden and Eldredge, 1947).
Nielsen, Niels C., *God in Education: A New Opportunity for
    American Schools* (New York: Sheed and Ward, 1966).
Nordstrom, Carl, Edgar Friedenberg, and Hillary Gold, *Society's
    Children: A Study of Resentment in the Secondary School*
    (New York: Random House, 1967).
Pfeffer, Leo, *Church, State, and Freedom* (Boston: Beacon Press,
    1967).
Phenix, Philip H., *Education and the Worship of God* (Philadelphia:
    The Westminister Press, 1966).
Politella, Joseph, ed., *Religion in Education: An Annotated
    Bibliography* (Oneonta, New York: American Association
    of Colleges for Teacher Education, 1956).
Raths, James, and Jean D. Grambs, eds., *Society and Education:
    Readings* (Englewood Cliffs: Prentice-Hall, 1965).
*Report of Conference on Religious Education and the Public
    School* (New York: Synagogue Council of America, 1944).
Rideman, Peter, *Account of Our Religion* (London: Hodder and
    Stoughton, Ltd., 1965).
Rodgers, Harrell Ross, Jr., *Community Conflict, Public Opinion
    and the Law: The Amish Dispute in Iowa* (Columbus, Ohio:
    C. E. Merrill Publishing Company, 1969).
Ryan, Mary P., *Are Parochial Schools the Answer?* (New York:
    Holt, Rinehart and Winston, 1964).
Sanders, Thomas, *Protestant Concepts of Church and State:
    Historical Backgrounds and Approaches for the Future*
    (New York: Doubleday, 1965).

Schreiber, William I., *Our Amish Neighbors* (Chicago: University of Chicago Press, 1962).

Seyfert, Ella Mail, *Little Amish Schoolhouse* (New York: Thomas Crowell, 1939).

Shelly, Paul Rickert, *Religious Education and Mennonite Piety Among the Mennonites of Southeastern Pennsylvania, 1870-1943* (North Newton, Kansas: Mennonite Publication Office, 1950).

Shirk, Eli M., *To the Members of the General Assembly of the Commonwealth of Pennsylvania* (Ephrata, Pennsylvania: Eli M. Shirk, 1941).

Simons, Menno, *The Complete Writings of Menno Simons* (Scottdale, Pennsylvania: Herald Press, 1956).

Smith, Elmer L., *The Amish Today: An Analysis of their Beliefs, Behavior and Contemporary Problems* (Allentown: Pennsylvania German Folklore Society, 1961).

Sperry, Willard L., *Religion and Education* (Cambridge: Harvard University Press, 1945).

Steinhiller and Soktlowski, *State Law on Compulsory Attendance* (Washington, D.C.: U.S. Department of Health, Education, and Welfare, 1966).

Stokes, Anson Phelps, and Leo Pfeffer, *Church and State in the United States* (New York: Harper and Row, 1964).

Stoll, Joseph D., ed., *The Challenge of the Child: Selections from the Blackboard Bulletin, 1957-1966*, second edition revised (Aylmer, Ontario, Canada: Pathway Publishing Corporation, 1967).

————, *Who Shall Educate Our Children?* (Aylmer, Ontario, Canada: Pathway Publishing Corporation, 1965).

Thayer, V. T., *Religion in Public Education* (New York: Viking Press, 1947).

Tips for Teachers: A Handbook for Amish Teachers (Aylmer, Ontario, Canada: Pathway Publishing Corporation, 1970).

Troeltsch, Ernst, *The Social Teaching of the Christian Churches* (New York: The Macmillan Press, 1931).

Umble, John S., *Ohio Mennonite Sunday Schools* (Goshen, Indiana: The Mennonite Historical Society, 1941).

Wells, Richard D., *Articles of Agreement Regarding the Indiana Amish Parochial Schools and Department of Public Instruction* (Indianapolis: Department of Public Instruction, 1967).

Welter, Rush, *Popular Education and Democratic Thought in America* (New York: Columbus Press, 1962).

Wenger, John C., *The Doctrines of the Mennonites* (Scottdale, Pennsylvania: Mennonite Publishing House, 1958).

—————, *Glimpses of Mennonite History and Doctrine* (Scottdale, Pennsylvania: Herald Press, 1949).

Whiting, Beatrice B., ed., *Six Cultures: Studies of Child Rearing* (New York: John Wiley and Sons, 1963).

Yoder, Gideon G., *The Nurture and Evangelism of Children* (Scottdale, Pennsylvania: Herald Press, 1959).

II.   ARTICLES:

Adams, Melvin W., "The Real Question in Iowa," *Liberty*, 61 (May-June, 1966), 7-11ff.

"The Agony of the Amish: Exodus from America?," *School and Society*, 100 (Summer, 1972), 281-282.

"The Amish," *Saturday Review*, 55 (June 24, 1972), 49.

"The Amish Affair and Religious Liberty," *The Christian Century*, 83 (April 13, 1966), 468-472.

"Amish, Black Muslims and Catholics," *America*, 116 (April 15, 1967), 550.

"The Amish Case," *Commonweal*, 96 (August 11, 1972), 419ff.

"Amish Case Appeal Causes Conflicting Emotions," *Liberty*, 66 (September-October, 1971), 30.

"Amish and Compulsory School Attendance: Recent Developments," *Wisconsin Law Review*, 832 (1971).

"The Amish Ruling and Religious Liberty," *Church and State*, 25 (July-August, 1972), 6-7.

"Amish: Tilting at Orange Triangles," *Christian Century*, 85 (November 20, 1968), 1466-1467.

"Amish Win Important Court Decision: Question of Compulsory School Attendance," *Christian Century*, 88 (January 27, 1971), 95.

Arons, Stephen, "Compulsory Education: The Plain People Resist," *Saturday Review*, 55 (January 15, 1972), 52-57.

Baehr, Karl, "Secularization Among the Mennonites of Elkhart County, Indiana," *The Mennonite Quarterly Review*, 16 (July, 1942), 131-160.

"The Balancing Process for Free Exercise Needs a New Scale," *North Carolina Law Review*, 51 (December, 1972), 302.

Ball, William, "Law and Religion in America: The New Picture," *Catholic Law*, 3 (1970), 16.

——, "Religion in Education: A Basis for Consensus," *America*, 108 (1963), 528.

Basinski, Anthony J., "The Amish Exemption: A Constitutionally Compelled Exemption," *University of Pittsburgh Law Review*, 34 (Winter, 1972), 275.

Bender, Harold S., trans and ed., "Some Early American Amish-Mennonite Disciplines," *Mennonite Quarterly Review*, 8, No. 2 (April, 1934), 90-98.

Berns, W., "Ratiocinations: Religion and Exemption from the Law," *Harper's*, 246 (March, 1973), 36ff.

Bontreger, Eli J., "What is a Good Education?," *The Challenge of the Child*, ed. Joseph Stoll (Aylmer, Ontario, Canada: Pathway Publishing Corporation, 1967).

Bossing, Nelson L., "The History of Educational Legislation in Ohio from 1851 to 1925," *Ohio Archeological and Historical Society Publications*, 39 (1930), 86.

Buchanan, F. S., "Secular Schoolmen and Amish Aims," *School and Society*, 97 (February, 1969), 104-105.

——, "Yoder Case: Precedent for Polygamy?," *Christian Century*, 90 (February 21, 1973), 223-224.

Buchicchio, Michael, "The Compulsory School Attendance Case,' *Akron Law Review*, 6 (Winter, 1973), 95.

Calhoun, John William, "The State's Case: Compulsory Education Immunizes Against the Disease of Ignorance," *Saturday Review*, 55 (January 15, 1972), 52-58.

Canty, Rosezella E., "Wisconsin v. Yoder, 406 U.S. 205 (1972)," *Duquesne Law Review*, 11 (Spring, 1973), 433.

Carley, W., "Parental Rights Under Fire," *Catholic World*, 189 (May, 1959), 137-142.

Casad, Robert C., "Compulsory Education and Individual Rights," *Religion and the Public Order*, ed. Donald Gianella (Chicago: University of Chicago Press, 1963).

——, "Compulsory High School Attendance and the Old Order Amish: A Commentary on State v. Garber," *University of Kansas Law Review*, 16 (April, 1968), 423-435.

Castelli, Jim, "Catholics and the Amish," *Commonweal*, 96 (June 16, 1972), 331-332.

Clark, John, "Guidelines for the Free Exercise Clause," *Harvard Law Review*, 83 (1969), 327, 344.

"Compulsory School Attendance Law: State Interests Balanced
    Against Beliefs of Members of the Amish Faith," *Washington
    Law Review*, 47 (1972), 331.
"Congress Responds to Amish Plight," *Christian Century*, 79
    (June 21, 1961), 765.
"Defining Religion: Of God, the Constitution and the D.A.R.,"
    University of Chicago Law Review, 32 (1965), 533, 548.
"Directory of [Amish] Schools and Teachers, 1966-67," *The
    Blackboard Bulletin*, 10 (November, 1966), 79-83.
"Educational Freedom for the Amish," *School and Society*, 95
    (December 9, 1967), 486-488.
"Eighth-Grade Education Enough for Amish Children," *American
    Bar Association Journal*, 58 (July, 1972), 747.
Engle, T. L., "An Analysis of Themes on the Subject of War
    as Written by Amish and Non-Amish Children," *The
    Journal of Educational Psychology*, 35 (May, 1944), 267-273.
————, "Attitudes Towards War as Expressed by Amish and
    Non-Amish Children: A Follow-Up Study," *Elementary
    School Journal*, 53 (February, 1953), 345-351.
————, "Personality Adjustments of Children Belonging to
    Two Minority Groups," *The Journal of Educational
    Psychology*, 36 (December, 1945), 543-560.
Erickson, Donald A., "On the Role of Nonpublic Schools,"
    School Review, 69 (Autumn, 1961), 338-353.
————, "The 'Plain People' and American Democracy,"
    Commentary, 45 (January, 1968), 36-44.
————, "The Plain People vs. the Common Schools," *Saturday
    Review*, 49 (November 19, 1966), 85-87ff.
————, "Showdown at an Amish Schoolhouse: A Description
    and Analysis of the Iowa Controversy," *Public Controls for
    Nonpublic Schools*, ed. Donald A. Erickson (Chicago:
    University of Chicago Press, 1969), 15-59.
————, "Storm Front: State Regulation of Nonpublic Schools,"
    Liberty, 62 ((November-December, 1967), 19-22ff.
Everett, G. D., "Amish Education and Religious Freedom,"
    Christianity Today, 16 (June 9, 1972), 15-18.
"Free Exercise of Religion vs. Compulsory Education," *Minnesota
    Law Review*, 56 (November, 1971), 111.
"Freedom of Religion: Amish Exempted from Wisconsin
    Compulsory Education Statute," *Valparaiso University Law
    Review*, 5 (Spring, 1971), 666.

"First Amendment Freedom of Religion and Compulsory Education
   Statute," *Notre Dame Law Review*, 48 (Fall, 1971), 136, 140.

"First Amendment Violated by Compulsory Education Statute
   that Prevents a Parent from Raising His Children According
   to Religious Beliefs," *Vanderbilt Law Review*, 24 (May,
   1971), 808.

Galanter, "Religious Freedoms in the United States: A Turning
   Point," *Wisconsin Law Review* (1966), 217, 265.

Gasho, Milton, "The Amish Division of 1693-1697 in Switzerland
   and Alsace," *Mennonite Quarterly Review* (October, 1937),
   235-266.

Giannella, Donald A., "Religious Liberty, Nonestablishment, and
   Doctrinal Development, Part I: The Religious Liberty
   Guarantee," *Harvard Law Review*, 80 (1967), 1381.

———, "Religious Liberty, Nonestablishment, and Doctrinal
   Development, Part II: The Nonestablishment Principle,"
   Harvard Law Review, 81 (January, 1968), 513.

Goldfine, J., "Defense of LeRoy Garber," *School Review*, 78
   (November, 1969), 91-103.

Gross, Neal, "Cultural Variables in Rural Communities," *The
   American Journal of Sociology*, 53 (March, 1948), 344-350.

Gutkind, Peter C. W., "Amish Acculturation," *American
   Anthropologist*, 60 (April, 1958).

Hertzler, Silas, "Mennonite Education Today," *School and Society*,
   80 (August 21, 1954), 59-60.

———, "Mennonite Elementary Schools 1947-1948," *Mennonite
   Quarterly Review*, 23 (January, 1949), 108-113.

Haight, James T., "The Amish School Controversy," *Ohio Bar
   Association Report*, 31 (October 6, 1958), 846-859.

Herrick, David J., "Religious Freedom and Compulsory Education:
   The Plight of the Amish," *South Dakota Law Review*,
   17 (Winter, 1972), 251.

Herringen, Jochem von, and Thomas McCorkle, "Culture and
   Medical Behavior of the Old Order Amish of Johnson County,
   Iowa," *State University of Iowa Institute of Medicine
   Bulletin*, No. 2 (1958).

Holliday, Albert E., "The Amish and Compulsory Education,"
   The Education Digest, 37 (May, 1972), 21-23.

Hostetler, John A., "The Amish, Citizens of Heaven and America,"
   Pennsylvania Folklore, 10 (Spring, 1959), 33-37.

————, "Amish Problems at Diener-Versammlungen," *Mennonite Life*, 34 (1949), 34-38.

————, "Amish Socialization Study," *Mennonite Quarterly Review*, 42 (January, 1968), 68-73.

————, "The Amish Use of Symbols and Their Function in Bounding the Community," *The Journal of the Royal Anthropological Institute*, 94 (1963), 11-22.

————, "The Life and Times of Samuel Yoder, 1824-1884," *Mennonite Quarterly Review* (October, 1948), 226-241.

————, "Old Order Amish Child Rearing and Schooling Practices," *Mennonite Quarterly Review*, 44 (April, 1970), 181-191.

————, "Old World Extinction and New World Survival of the Amish," *Rural Sociology* (September-December, 1955).

————, "Persistence and Change Patterns in Amish Society," *Ethnology*, 3, No. 2 (April, 1964), 185-198.

————, "Socialization and Adaptations to Public Schooling: The Hutterian Brethren and the Old Order Amish," *Social Quarterly*, 11 (Spring, 1970), 194-205.

————, "The Surprising Amish," *Saturday Review*, 55 (March 4, 1972), 16.

Hostetler, John A., and Calvin Redekop, "Education and Assimilation in Three Ethnic Groups," *Alberta Journal of Educational F   ʻh, 8, No. 4 (December, 1962).

Knight, David M., "State Regulation of Independent Schools," *America*, 93 (June 4, 1956), 263-265.

Kollmorgen, Walter M., "The Agricultural Stability of the Old Order Amish and Old Order Mennonites of Lancaster County, Pennsylvania," *The American Journal of Sociology*, 49 (November, 1943), 233-241.

Kuhn, Manford H., "Factors in Personality: Socio-Cultural Determinants as Seen Through the Amish," *Aspects of Culture and Personality*, ed. Francis Hsu (New York: Abelard-Schuman, 1954), 43.

Kurokawa, M., "Acculturation and Mental Health of Mennonite Children," *Child Development*, 40 (September, 1969), 689-705.

Landing, J. E., "Amish, the Automobile, and Social Interaction," *Journal of Geography*, 71 (January, 1972), 52-57.

Leatherman, Quintus, "Christopher Dock, Mennonite Schoolmaster, 1718-1771," *Mennonite Quarterly Review*, 16 (January, 1942), 34-44.

Lembright, M. L., and K. Yamamoto, "Subcultures and Creative
    Thinking: An Exploratory Comparison Between Amish and
    Urban American School Children," *Merrill-Palmer Quarterly
    of Behavior and Development*, 11 (1965), 49-64.
Lindholm, William C., "Kansas v. Garber," *Liberty*, 62 (September-
    October, 1967), 17-20.
————, "Let the Amish Live in Peace," *Liberty*, 65 (July-August,
    1970), 22-25.
Littell, Franklin H., "The State of Iowas vs. the Amish," *The
    Christian Century*, 83 (February 23, 1966), 234-235ff.
Loomis, Charles P., and Carl R. Jantzen, "Boundary Maintenance
    vs. Systematic Linkage in School Integration: The Case of
    the Amish in the United States," *The Journal of the
    Pakistan Academy for Village Development*, 3, No. 2
    (October, 1962), 1-25.
Massinari, Karl, "The Contribution of Christopher Dock to
    Contemporary Christian Teaching," *Mennonite Quarterly
    Review*, 15 (April, 1951), 100-115.
Miller, Anita Leslie, "Amish Granted Exemption to State Statute
    Requiring Secondary Education to Age Sixteen,"
    Cumberland-Samford Law Review, 3 (Fall, 1972), 508.
Miller, Harvey J., "Proceedings of Amish Ministers Conferences
    1826-31," *Mennonite Quarterly Review* (April, 1959),
    132-142.
"Past and Present Clash in Wisconsin," *Liberty*, 65 (March-April,
    1970), 8-10.
Pfeffer, Leo, "Religion in the Upbringing of Children," *Boston
    University Law Review*, 35 (1955), 333.
Prance, Norman R., "Amish and Compulsory School Attendance:
    Recent Developments," *Wisconsin Law Review*, 832 (1971).
Pratt, W. F., "Anabaptist Explosion: Adaptation of Pockets of
    High Fertility in the United States," *Natural History*, 78
    (February, 1969), 8-10ff.
Reed, Thomas J., "The Amish—A Case Study in Accommodation
    and Suppression," *Notre Dame Lawyer*, 43 (June, 1968),
    764-776.
"Religious Freedom," *U.S. Congressional Record* (December 9,
    1971), S21007-S21011.
"Religious Garb in the Public Schools—A Study in Conflicting
    Liberties," *University of Chicago Law Review*, 22 (1955),
    888.

"Religious Groups Support Amish in Court Battle," *Liberty*, 67 (January-February, 1972), 25-26.

Roper, William L., "The Plight of the Plain People," *Liberty*, 59 (March-April, 1964), 8-11.

Ruxin, Paul T., "The Right Not to be Modern Men: The Amish and Compulsory Education," *Virginia Law Review*, 53 (May, 1967), 925-952.

Ryder, H. E., "The Problem of the Amish as Related to School Attendance," *School and Society*, 23 (January 2, 1926), 17.

Saladin, Peter R., "Relative Ranking of the Preferred Freedoms: Religion and Speech," *Religion and the Public Order*, ed. Donald Gianella (Chicago: University of Chicago Press, 1963).

Seminara, Robert J., "Amish Parents Not Required to Enroll Children in Secondary School," *Notre Dame Lawyer*, 48 (February, 1973), 741.

Simons, Menno, "Christians and Their Children," *The Blackboard Bulletin* (April, 1968).

Sky, Theodore, "The Establishment Clause, the Congress and the Schools: An Historical Perspective," *Virginia Law Review*, 52 (1966), 1395.

Stahmer, Harold, "Defining Religion: Federal Aid and Academic Freedom," *Religion and the Public Order*, ed. Donald Gianella (Chicago: University of Chicago Press, 1963).

"State v. Hershberger," *The Ohio Bar*, 30 (September 16, 1957), 188-193.

Stephens, H. M., "School, Church and State," *Marquette Law Review*, 12 (April, 1928), 206-231.

Stoll, Joseph, "Fireside Chats Number 3—In Which are Discussed Hogs and Highmindedness," *The Blackboard Bulletin*, 10 (February, 1967), 141-144.

Tortora, Vincent R., "The Amish in Their One-Room Schoolhouses," *Pennsylvania Folklore*, 11 (Fall, 1960), 42-46.

"Using the Amish," *Christianity Today*, 16 (January 7, 1972), 26-27.

Van Alstyne, William, "Constitutional Separation of Church and State: The Quest for a Coherent Position," *American Political Science Review*, 57 (1963), 865, 873.

Wagler, David, "Education, a Grave Responsibility," *The Blackboard Bulletin* (January, 1963).

Wallace, Allen F., "The Amish and Their Right to Reject
    Compulsory School Attendance Beyond the Eighth Grade,"
    Mercer Law Review, 24 (Winter, 1973), 479.

Walsh, Edward J., Jr., "Free Exercise Clause Prohibits Compulsory
    Education of Amish Children," *Loyola University Law
    Journal*, 4 (Winter, 1973), 256.

Weiss, Arthur, "Amish Religion vs. State Interest in Education,"
    Journal of Urban Law, 50 (February, 1973), 493.

Weiss, Jonathan, "Privilege, Posture, and Protection–'Religion' in
    the Law," *Yale Law Journal*, 73 (1964), 593, 609.

"Wisconsin's Compulsory School Attendance Law as Applied to
    Members of the Amish Religion Violates Their Rights
    Under the Free Exercise Clause of the First Amendment,"
    Georgetown Law Journal, 61 (October, 1972), 236.

"Wisconsin v. Yoder: The Right to be Different–First Amendment
    Exemption for Amish Under the Free Exercise Clause,"
    De Paul Law Review, 22 (Winter, 1972), 539.

Wittmer, Joe, "Homogeneity of Personality Characteristics:
    A Comparison Between Old Order Amish and Non-Amish,"
    American Anthropology, 72 (October, 1970), 1063-1068.

————, "An Educational Controversy: The Old Order Amish
    Schools," *Phi Delta Kappan*, 52 (November, 1970), 142-145.

————, "Plight of the Old Order Amish," *Current Anthropology*,
    12 (February, 1971), 106.

————, "Amish Schools Today," *School and Society*, 99
    (April, 1971), 227-230.

————, "Cultural Violence and Twentieth Century Progress,"
    Practical Anthropology, 18 (July-August, 1971), 146-155.

Wolterstorff, Nicholas, "The Amish in Court," *The Reformed
    Journal* (July-August, 1972), 23.

Yoder, John Howard, "Caesar and the Meidung," *The Mennonite
    Quarterly Review* (April, 1949), 76-98.

Zajac, S. A., "Going to the Heart of the Amish Question,"
    Michigan Education Journal, 43 (May, 1966), 22-23.

III.   THESES:

Billings, T. A., "The Old Order Amish Versus the Compulsory
    School Attendance Laws (Ph.D. dissertation, University of
    Oregon, 1961).

Buchanan

Buchanan, Frederick, "The Old Paths: A Study of the Amish Response to Public Schooling in Ohio" (Ph.D. dissertation, Ohio State University, 1967).

Getz, Jane C., "Religious Forces in the Economic and Social Life of the Old Order Amish in Lancaster County, Pennsylvania" (M.A. thesis, American University, 1945).

Gutkind, Peter C. W., "Secularization vs. the Christian Community: The Problems of an Old Order House Amish Family" (M.A. thesis, University of Chicago, 1952).

Harder, Menno S., "The Origin, Philosophy and Development of Education Among the Mennonites" (Ph.D. dissertation, University of Southern California, 1959).

Hayes, Donald P., "The Iowa Amish and Their Education" (Ph.D. dissertation, University of Iowa, 1972).

Huntington, Abbie Gertrude Enders, "Dove at the Window: A Study of an Old Order Amish Community in Ohio" (Ph.D. dissertation, Yale University, 1956).

Madeira, Sheldon, "A Study of the Education of the Old Order Mennonites of Lancaster County, Pennsylvania" (Ph.D. dissertation, University of Pennsylvania, 1955).

Miller, D. Paul, "Amish Acculturation" (M.A. thesis, University of Nebraska, 1949).

Miller, Wayne, "A Study of Amish Academic Achievement" (Ph.D. dissertation, University of Michigan, 1969).

Mitchell, Frederic, "The Supreme Court of the United States on Religion and Education (1844-1948)" (Ph.D. dissertation, Columbia University, 1959).

Osborn, R. L., "Patterns of Separation of Church and State in Relation to Education" (Ph.D. dissertation, Indiana University, 1961).

Smith, Elmer L., "A Study of Acculturation in an Amish Community" (Ph.D. dissertation, Syracuse University, 1955).

Stoltzfus, Grant M., "History of the First Amish Mennonite Communities in America" (M.A. thesis, University of Pittsburgh, 1954).

Wittmer, Joe, "A Comparison of the Variability of Perceived Parental Behavior Characteristics and Personality Traits of Twenty-Five Non-Amish and Twenty-Five Amish Male Youth, Between the Ages of 18 and 20, From the Same Community" (Ph.D. dissertation, Indiana State University, 1968).

Yoder, John Paul, "Social Isolation Devices in an Amish-
    Mennonite Community" (M.A. thesis, State College, 1941).
Yutzy, Daniel, "The Changing Amish: An Inter-generational Study"
    (M.A. thesis, Ohio State University, 1961).

IV.   UNPUBLISHED MATERIAL:

Buchanan, Frederick S., The Amish Concept of the Child as
    Reflected in *The Blackboard Bulletin*, 1968.
Byler, Uria R., Testimony Before the Amish School Study
    Committee, Columbus, Ohio: Ohio Legislative Service
    Commission, November 22, 1960.
Dush, Joseph, Testimony Before the Amish School Study
    Committee, Columbus, Ohio: Ohio Legislative Service
    Commission, November 22, 1960.
Erickson, Donald A., The Amish and the State School Statutes:
    A Position Paper, read at the Midwestern State Attorneys
    General Detroit Conference, December 5-7, 1965.
Gallagher, Helene, Amish and Control Group Children's Drawings
    Analyzed Through Psychological Techniques, 1969.
Hostetler, John A., Anabaptist Conceptions of Child Nurture
    and Schooling: A Collection of Source Materials Used by
    the Old Order Amish, 1968.
Kelley, Dean, Religious Liberty and the Old Order Amish, 1966.
Lindholm, William C., Religious Liberty Defined: Some
    Implications—The Amish and Their Schools, East Tawas,
    Michigan, March, 1966.
McCorkle, Thomas, Cultural Persistence and the Iowa Amish,
    proceedings of the Fifth International Congress of
    Anthropologists and Ethnologists, Philadelphia, Pennsylvania,
    1956.
Munro, Edith, Amish-Mennonite Schools in the State of Iowa,
    report to the State Board of Public Instruction, Des Moines,
    Iowa, January 13, 1972.
Ohio Legislative Service Commission, Amish Sectarian Education in
    Ohio. Research Report No. 44 (research staff: James M.
    Furman, Research Associate; Ann M. Erickson, Research
    Attorney; Lauren A. Glosser, Director), Columbus, Ohio,
    December, 1960.
Ohio Legislative Service Commission, minutes of Amish School
    Study Committee, August 18, 1960.

Ohio State Department of Education, A Study of the Public Schools of Geauga County with Recommendations for their Future Organization, Columbus, Ohio State Department of Education, 1937.

Pennsylvania Department of Public Instruction, Policy for Operation of Home and Farm Projects in Church Organized Schools, Harrisburg, Pennsylvania, October 5, 1955.

Purches, Janice, An Analysis of Amish Children's Drawings, 1969.

Shirk, Eli M., ed., Report of Committee of Plain People Making Pleas for Leniency From Depressive School Laws, Ephrata, Pennsylvania, 1939.

————, History of Our Controversy, Ephrata, Pennsylvania, 1959.

Statement of Policy by the Council of Amish Bishops and the Amish Committee of Education, released February 22, 1950.

Stoltzfus, Stephen F., et al., To Our Men of Authority, Bird-in-Hand, Pennsylvania, November 17, 1937.

Swartz, Alan M., Cross-Cultural Studies of Amish, Negro, and White Children by the Analysis of Drawings and Occupational Aspirations, 1969.

Wenger, Raymond, ed., Compulsory Attendance Law Versus Religious Liberty Provision, 1970-71.

Wisconsin Legislature Council, Staff Report to the Education Committee on the Amish Community in Wisconsin and Selected Other States, 1968.

V. COLLECTIONS:

Source materials on the Amish and education, the Amish and Social Security, and conscientious objection to war are located in the Menno Simons Historical Library, Eastern Mennonite College, Harrisonburg, Virginia.

Index

Adult baptism: 101, 103, 117
Age, school-leaving: 1, 13, 78, 85, 86, 108, 137
Agricultural enterprise: 2, 55, 76
Alley, Robert J.: 13-14
Alsace: 4-5
American Association for Advancement of Atheism: 37
American School: 86
Amish education: agrarianism and, 11; Bible in, 23-24, 28; content, 108; criticism of, 56; objectives of, 3, 25, 31, 58-59, 77, 101, 127, 130
Amish movement: Anabaptists and, 3-7; history of, 1-15; Mennonites and, 5-6, 9-10; progressives and conservatives, 10-11; schism of 1693, 7, 9
Amish schools: comparing to public schools, 79, 80-83; elementary level, 78; exemptions for, 78; location of, 107; primitive conditions of, 58-60; teachers in, 108
Amish society: adult baptism, 101, 103, 117; communal aspects, 6-7, 76, 107-108; dress codes, 8, 31, 141; educational goals, 3, 25, 31, 58, 77, 101, 106; enforcement of discipline, 4, 8-9, 46, 101, 103, 104; family, 7, 14, 56, 111; group discipline, 5, 76, 101, 104; importance of community in, 7, 9, 14, 130; language, 2, 9, 25; parents role in, 14-19,

22, 28, 46, 105, 133; preserving, 76; religion in, 18-19, 24, 36, 117-118; resistance to assimilation, 7-8, 54, 77, 80, 90, 106; respect for tradition, 14, 80, 117; self-sufficiency in, 2, 55, 77, 87; separatism of, 76, 101, 102-103, 105; simplicity, 8, 58; and socialization, 101-108, 130; view of nature, 105; within the larger society, 54-56, 76, 81, 87, 106, 111-113, 128; young in, 77, 81-82, 91, 105
Amish Society (Hostetler): 125
Amman, Jacob: 5-6, 10, 104
Anabaptist Vision: 3-4, 6
Anabaptists: Amish schism and, 7; and discipline, 104; education and, 20-21, 28, 106; formation of subgroups, 5-6; persecution of, 4, 20, 28; view of war, 102
Anderson, Melvin: 58-60, 62
Apple Grove School: 26-27
Arkansas: 91
Arons, Stephen: 124-135
Arthaud, C. J.: 53
Assimilation: dangers of, 77, 80, 90, 106; forced, 90; German language and, 9; resistance to, 6-8, 54, 77, 80, 90, 106
Atheism: 34, 36-37, 141
Attendance laws: early, 12, 23; exemption from, 79, 114-115, 120, 132, 146; socialization and, 101-108, 130-135; view of the courts, 12, 80, 126